Integrated Army Planning
Reference Guide

Second Edition

Buck Carroll

2016

"In preparing for battle I have always found that plans
are useless, but planning is indispensable."
General Dwight D. Eisenhower

Foreword

The purpose of this guide is to consolidate commonly used information for planning and place it in a guide that could fit in a cargo pocket. The source documents provide the depth, this guide provides instant accessible feedback.

This is an independent publication published by Buck Carroll. Use of military doctrine, symbols, graphics and/or materials in no way constitutes endorsement or collaboration by the Department of Defense or military services. The information in this reference guide is distributed on an "as is" basis, without warranty. While every precaution has been taken to ensure the reliability and accuracy of all data and contents, the author shall have no liability to any person or entity with respect to liability, loss or discrepancy. Any questions default to the source document. The views of this publication are those of the author and do not necessarily represent the views of the Department of Defense or its components.

Planning Insights

- Maintain constant dialogue both horizontally and vertically.
- Don't just admire the problem.
- Just accept the fact that the plan is always wrong.
- Remember that the plan is not yours, it's the commanders.
- You will fail if you don't plan to plan.
- Know how your commander visualizes information.
- Perfection is the enemy of good enough.
- When possible iterate to produce better products.
- Never shock the commander in a public forum, dialogue and read-aheads are essential.
- It's all about telling the story.
- If you have a question, ask it.
- Diverting from doctrine is acceptable but do it intentionally and be able to answer why.
- Always take notes when the commander speaks.
- First, identify what you know and then what you don't.
- Focus on options for the commander not on "the solution."
- There are three types of briefs: staff to staff, staff to commander, and your commander to his commander. All are important but don't use the wrong one.
- Don't present information you don't intend to brief.
- If you need information from others, provide a desired format.
- Don't bring a problem to the boss without possible solutions.
- Be aware of your biases.
- If you make a mistake, own up to it.
- Know yourself and be consistent, others can sense insincerity.
- Remember that graphic control measures are free.
- You must always question the "logical" way forward.

Table of Contents

Chapter 3 - Conceptual Planning

Chapter 4 – Model Playbook

Chapter 1 - General Reference

Elements of Decisive Action and Subordinate Tasks

Purpose: Every element within Decisive Action has specific subordinate tasks enabling completion.

Origin: ADRP 3-90 (AUG12)

OFFENSE	DEFENSE
Movement to Contact • Search and Attack • Cordon and Search	Area Defense
Attack • Ambush • Counterattack • Demonstration • Spoiling Attack • Feint • Raid	Retrograde operations • Delay • Withdrawal • Retirement
Exploitation	Mobile Defense
Pursuit	

STABILITY	DEFENSE SUPPORT TO CIVIL AUTHORITIES
Civil Security	Provide Support for Domestic Disasters
Civil Control	Provide support for Domestic Chemical, Biological, Radiological, and Nuclear Incidents
Restore Essential Services	Provide Support to Domestic Civilian Law Enforcement Agencies
Support To Governance	Provide Other Designated

	Support
Support to Economic and Infrastructure Development	

Forms of Maneuver/Defense

Purpose: While not tactical tasks, decisive action contains specific forms of maneuver and defense.

Origin: ADRP 3-90 (AUG12)

Forms of Maneuver	Forms of Defense
Envelopment	Defense of a Linear Obstacle
Flank Attack	Perimeter Defense
Frontal Attack	Reverse Slope Defense
Infiltration	
Penetration	
Turning Movement	

Tactical Enabling Tasks

Purpose: Tactical enabling tasks enable the completion of the broader subordinate tasks of decisive action.

Origin: ADRP 3-90 (AUG12)

Security Operations	Reconnaissance Operations
Screen	Zone
Guard	Area
Cover	Route
Area (includes route and convoy)	Recon in Force
Local	

Mobility Operations	Troop Movement
Breaching Operations	Administrative Movement
Clearing Operations	Approach March
Gap-Crossing Operations	Road March
Combat Roads and Trails	
Forward Airfields and Landing Zones	
Traffic Operations	

Encirclement Operations	Relief in Place
Passage of Lines	

Purpose Words

Purpose: This table consolidates sample purpose verbs for "in order to" phrases in mission statements. While they're labeled as "sample" most consider them doctrinal. This table is not found in recent doctrinal publications.

Origin: FM 5-0.1 (MAR06)

Purpose	
Allow	Envelop
Cause	Influence
Create	Open
Deceive	Protect
Deny	Prevent
Divert	Support
Enable	Surprise

Tactical Mission Task Symbols

Purpose: This table contains the current tactical mission tasks and their symbols.

Task	Symbol **Note:** The friendly or hostile frame (gray) is not part of the symbol; it is for orientation only.
Breach	B
Bypass	B
Canalize	C
Clear	— C →
Contain	C
Control	C
Counterattack	CATK / A
Counterattack by fire	CATK
Delay or delay (until a specific time)	W / ← D
Demonstration	← DEM

Task	Symbol *Note:* The friendly or hostile frame (gray) is not part of the symbol; it is for orientation only.
Destroy	
Disengage/disengagement	DIS
Disrupt	D
Envelopment	E
Exfiltrate	EX
Exploit	
Feint	
Fix	F
Follow and assume	A
Follow and support	A
Infiltration/infiltrate	IN

Task	Symbol **Note:** The friendly or hostile frame (gray) is not part of the symbol; it is for orientation only.
Interdict	I
Isolate	
Neutralize	N
Occupy	O
Passage of lines (forward)	P(F)
Passage of lines (rearward)	P(R)
Penetration/penetrate	P
Relief in place	RIP
Retain	R
Retirement	R

Task	Symbol *Note*: The friendly or hostile frame (gray) is not part of the symbol; it is for orientation only.
Secure	

Security
Note: Unit to perform security is placed in the center of symbol.

Type	Icon
Security (screen)	S
Security (cover)	C
Security (guard)	G
Seize	
Support by fire	
Suppress	
Turn	
Withdraw	
Withdraw under pressure	

Task	Symbol Note: The friendly or hostile frame (gray) is not part of the symbol; it is for orientation only.
Ambush	
Attack by fire	
Block	B

Combat Power Planning Ratios

Purpose: While not doctrinal, these are traditional planning ratios. They indicate the required combat power to achieve parity.

Origin: CALL Staff Officer's Quick Reference Guide (2013)

Friendly Mission	Position	Friendly:Enemy
Delay		1:5
Defend	Prepared/Fortified	1:3
Defend	Hasty	1:2.5
Attack	Prepared/Fortified	3:1
Attack	Hasty	2.5:1
Counterattack	Flank	1:1
Counterinsurgency		20:1,000 (residents)

Purpose: The chart provides weather analysis for intelligence preparation and mission planning.
Origin: TC 2-50-5 (JAN10)

Mission	Element	Favorable (Unrestricted	Marginal (Restricted)	Unfavorable (Severely Restricted)
Mobility (track, day)	Visibility	>1.5K	0.8 to 1.5K	<0.8K
	Rainfall	<0.1IN/H	0.1 to 0.5K/H	>0.5K/H
	Snow Depth	<12IN	12 to 20IN	>20IN
Mobility (track, night)	Visibility	>0.2K	0.1 to 0.2K	<0.1K
	Rainfall	<0.1IN/H	0.1 to 0.5IN/H	>0.5IN/H
	Snow Depth	>12IN	12 to 20IN	>20IN
Mobility (dismount)	Visibility	>0.3K	0.1 to 0.3K	<0.1K
	Rainfall	<0.1IN/H	0.1 to 0.5IN/K	>0.5K/H
	Snow Depth	<3IN	3 to 6IN	>6IN
	Temperature	<32C	>32C	<-30C
	Wind-chill	>0C	0C to -30C	<-30C
Weapons Positioning	Visibility	>3.0K	0.5 to 3.0K	<0.5K
	Temperature	>18C	<-18C	
Fires Support (155M)	Visibility	>5.0K	1.5 to 5.0K	<1.5K
	Ceiling	>800FT	500 to 800 FT	<500FT
	Surface Wind	<35Knots	35 to 50 Knots	>50Knots
	Snow Depth	<4.0IN	4.0 to 6.0IN	>6IN
Smoke	Precipitation	None	Light	Moderate
Airborne (FW)	Visibility	>5K	1 to 5K	<1.0K
	Ceiling	>500FT	300 to 500FT	<300FT
	Surface Wind	<10Knots	10 to 13 Knots	>13Knots
	Precipitation	None	Light	Freezing
Aviation (RW)	Visibility	>1.5K	0.4 to 1.5K	<0.4K
	Ceiling	>500FT	300 to 500FT	<300FT
	Surface Wind	<20Knots	20 to 30 Knots	>30 Knots
	Precipitation	None	Light	Freezing

Rates of Advance

Purpose: The chart enables calculation of unit movement times.
Origin: MSTP Pamphlet 5-0.2 (MAY12)

Division Opposed Rates of Advance (km/day)												
Degree of Resistance	Prepared Defense (Note 5)						Hasty Defense (Note 6)					
Attacker : Defender Ration	Go Terrain		Slow Go Terrain		No Go Terrain		Go Terrain		Slow Go Terrain		No Go Terrain	
	Arm/Mech	Inf	Arm/Mech	Inf	Arm/Mech	Inf	Arm/Mech	Inf	Arm/Mech	Inf	Arm/Mech	Inf
Intense 1:1	2	2	1	1	0.6	0.6	4	4	2	2	1.21	1.2
Very Heavy 2:1 (-)	5 to 6	4	2 to 3	2	1.5 to 1.8	1.2	10 to 12	8	5 to 6	4	3 to 3.6	2.4
Heavy (3:1)	7 to 8	5	3 to 4	2.5	2.1 to 2.3	1.5	13 to 17	10	8	5	3.9 to 4.8	3
Medium (4:1)	8 to 10	6	4 to 5	3	2.4 to 3	1.8	16 to 20	12	10	6	4.8 to 6	3.6
Light (5:1)	16 to 20	10	8 to 10	5	4.8 to 6	3	30 to 40	18	20	9	9 to 12	5.4
Negligible (6:1)	24 to 30	12	12 to 15	6	7.2 to 9	3.6	48 to 60	24	30	12	14.4 to 18	7.2

Brigade and Below Opposed Rates of Advance (km/day)												
Degree of Resistance	Prepared Defense (Note 5)						Hasty Defense (Note 6)					
Attacker : Defender Ration	Go Terrain		Slow Go Terrain		No Go Terrain		Go Terrain		Slow Go Terrain		No Go Terrain	
	Arm/Mech	Inf	Arm/Mech	Inf	Arm/Mech	Inf	Arm/Mech	Inf	Arm/Mech	Inf	Arm/Mech	Inf
Intense 1:1	0.6	0.5	0.5	0.3	0.15	0.1	1	0.8	0.8	0.5	0.4	0.2
Very Heavy 2:1 (-)	0.9	0.6	0.6	0.4	0.3	0.2	1.5	1	1	0.7	0.6	0.3
Heavy (3:1)	1.2	0.7	0.75	0.5	0.5	0.3	2	1.2	1.3	0.9	0.8	0.5
Medium (4:1)	1.4	0.8	1	0.6	0.5	0.5	2.4	1.4	1.7	1.1	0.9	0.8
Light (5:1)	1.5	0.9	1.1	0.7	0.6	0.5	2.6	1.6	2	1.2	1	0.9
Negligible (6:1)	1.7+	1+	1.3+	0.8	0.6	0.6+	3+	1.7+	2.3+	1.3+	1.1+	1

Notes (both tables)
1. Brigade and below units can't sustain these rates for 24 hours.
2. The relative combat power ratio must be computed for the unit(s) under consideration.
3. When there is surprise, multiply these figures by a surprise factor as follows:
    - Complete Surprise x 5 (e.g. Germans at The Ardennes in 1944, Arabs in 1973)
    - Substantial Surprise x 3 (e.g. German Invasion of Russia in 1941, Israeli's Invasion of Sinai in 1967)
    - Minor Surprise x 1.3 (e.g. Allied Normandy landing in 1944, Pakistanis' attack on India in 1971)
4. The effects of surprise last for 3 days, being reduced by one-third on day 2 and two thirds on day 3.
5. Hasty defense is based on 2 to 12 hours of preparation time.
6. The ratios used here are to determine the degree of resistance. There is no direct relationship between advance rates and force ratios. However, sustained advances probably are not possible with a 3 to 1 ratio. Advance is possible against superior forces but can't be sustained.
7. Rates greater than 6 to 1 will result in advances between these and unopposed rates.

Planning Times/Days

Purpose: The chart alphabetically lists days/times for reference.
Origin: ATTP 5-0.1 (SEP11)

Term	Definition
C-Day	The unnamed day on which a deployment operation is to commence.
D-Day	The unnamed day on which a particular operation is to commence.
E-Day	The day on which a NATO exercise commences.
F-Hour	The effective time of announcement by the Secretary of Defense to the Military Departments of a Decision to mobilize Reserve units.
G-Day	The day on which a NATO order is given to deploy a unit.
H-Hour	The specific hour on D-day at which a particular operation commences.
L-Hour	The specific hour on C-day when the deployment commences.
M-Day	The unnamed day when the full mobilization commences
N-Day	The unnamed day an active duty unit is notified for deployment or redeployment.
O-Day	The day the MPSRON begins offload or the Fly-In Echelon commences.
P-Hour	The unnamed hour the first paratrooper exits the aircraft (non-doctrinal).
S-Day	The day the President authorizes Selective Reserve call up.
T-Day	The day of the Presidential declaration of national emergency or authorization of partial mobilization.

Fire Control Measures

Purpose: The chart consolidates fire control measures for planning.

Origin: Cavalry Leader's Course Reference Slides (2006)

Terrain-Based	Threat-Based
Target Reference Point (TRP)	Rules of Engagement (ROE)
Engagement Area (EA)	Weapons Ready Posture
Sector of Fire	Weapons Safety Posture
Direction of Fire	Weapons Control Status
Terrain-Base Quadrant	Engagement Priorities
Friendly-Based Quadrant	Trigger
Maximum Engagement Line	Engagement Techniques
Restrictive Fire Line (RFL)	Fire Patterns
Final Protective Line (FPL)	Target Array

Security Mission Dimensions

Purpose: The table provides average width/depth for security operations.

Origin: FM 3-90.2 (MAR13)

	ECHELON		
	HBCT	IBCT	SBCT
Screen			
Width	20-30 km	15-20 km	20-30 km
Depth	10-15 km	5-10 km	10-15 km
Guard (when augmented)			
Width	30-40 km		
Depth	20-30 km		
Area Security (sq km)	Up to 55 km		
Local/Area Security			
Route (Cordon)	6 combat outposts Approx 15-25 km of route	4 combat outposts Approx 10-20 km of route	9 combat outposts Approx 15-25 km of route
Convoy (20-25 vehicles)	3 convoys	2 convoys	3 convoys

Reconnaissance Guidance

Purpose: This traditional framework provides guidance for recon missions.
Origin: FM 3-90.96 (MAR10)

Guidance	Mission Variables	Execution Information
Focus	Enemy Terrain/Weather Civil Considerations	Commander's Intent Recon Objective Coordinating Instructions/Control Measures
Tempo	Mission Enemy Time Available	Planning Timeline Critical Tasks CCIR Tactical Risk Movement Techniques Recon Methods Formations
Engagement Criteria	Mission Enemy Troops/SPT Available Civil Considerations	Bypass Criteria Priorities of Fire Actions on Contact Recon Handover FSCM ROE Weapons Control Status Info Engagement

Joint/International Command Relationships

Purpose: The table outlines authorities based on relationships.
Origin: JP 5-0 (AUG11)

Authority	US COCOM	US OPCON	NATO OPCOM	NATO OPCON	CFC/USFK Combined OPCON	NATO TACOM	US & NATO TACOM
Direct authority to deal with DoD, US diplomatic missions, agencies	X						
Coordinate CINC boundary	X						
Granted by command	X		X				
Delegated to a command				X	X	X	X
Set chain of command to forces	X	X					
Assign mission/designate objective	X	X	X				
Assign tasks	X	X	X			X	
Direct/employ forces	X	X	X	X	X		
Establish maneuver control measures	X	X	X	X	X	X	X
Reassign forces	X		?				
Retain OPCON	X	X	X				
Delegate OPCON	X	X	X	X With approval			
Assign TACON	X	X					
Delegated TACON	X	X	X	X	X		
Retain TACON	X	X	X	X			
Deploy forces (information/within theater)	X	X	X	X			
Local direction/ control designated forces	X	X					X
Assign separate employment of unit components	X	X	X				
Directive authority for logistics	X						
Direct joint training	X	X					
Exercise command of US forces in MNF	X	X					
Assign/reassign subordinate commanders/officers	X	May suspend or recommend reassignment					
Conduct internal discipline/training	X						

NATO Full Command and CFC/USFK Command less OPCON are basically equivalent to US COCOM but only for internal matters.

Grey cells are either denied this authority or not specifically granted it.

COCOM-Combatant command
OPCON-Operational control
OPCOM-Operational command
TACOM-Tactical command
TACON-Tactical control

Army Command/Support Relationships

Purpose: The charts explain Army specific command and support relationships.

Origin: ADRP 5-0 (MAY12)

If relation-ship is:	**Then inherent responsibilities:**							
	Have command relation-ship with:	May be task-organized by:[1]	Unless modified, ADCON responsi-bility goes through:	Are assigned position or AO by:	Provide liaison to:	Establish/ maintain communi-cations with:	Have priorities establish-ed by:	Can impose on gaining unit further command or support relationship of:
Organic	All organic forces organized with the HQ	Organic HQ	Army HQ specified in organizing document	Organic HQ	N/A	N/A	Organic HQ	Attached; OPCON; TACON; GS; GSR; R; DS
Assigned	Combatant command	Gaining HQ	Gaining Army HQ	OPCON chain of command	As required by OPCON	As required by OPCON	ASCC or Service-assigned HQ	As required by OPCON HQ
Attached	Gaining unit	Gaining unit	Gaining Army HQ	Gaining unit	As required by gaining unit	Unit to which attached	Gaining unit	Attached; OPCON; TACON; GS; GSR; R; DS
OPCON	Gaining unit	Parent unit and gaining unit; gaining unit may pass OPCON to lower HQ[1]	Parent unit	Gaining unit	As required by gaining unit	As required by gaining unit and parent unit	Gaining unit	OPCON; TACON; GS; GSR; R; DS
TACON	Gaining unit	Parent unit	Parent unit	Gaining unit	As required by gaining unit	As required by gaining unit and parent unit	Gaining unit	TACON; GS GSR; R; DS

If relation-ship is:	**Then inherent responsibilities:**							
	Have command relation-ship with:	May be task-organized by:	Receives sustain-ment from:	Are assigned position or an area of operations by:	Provide liaison to:	Establish/ maintain communi-cations with:	Have priorities established by:	Can impose on gaining unit further command or support relation-ship by:
Direct support[1]	Parent unit	Parent unit	Parent unit	Supported unit	Supported unit	Parent unit; supported unit	Supported unit	See note[1]
Reinforc-ing	Parent unit	Parent unit	Parent unit	Reinforced unit	Reinforced unit	Parent unit; reinforced unit	Reinforced unit; then parent unit	Not applicable
General support–reinforc-ing	Parent unit	Parent unit	Parent unit	Parent unit	Reinforced unit and as required by parent unit	Reinforced unit and as required by parent unit	Parent unit; then reinforced unit	Not applicable
General support	Parent unit	Parent unit	Parent unit	Parent unit	As required by parent unit	As required by parent unit	Parent unit	Not applicable

Note: [1] Commanders of units in direct support may further assign support relationships between their subordinate units and elements of the supported unit after coordination with the supported commander.

Purpose: This diagram displays the organizations within aviation movement.

Origin: 2/1AD Aviation Smart Book

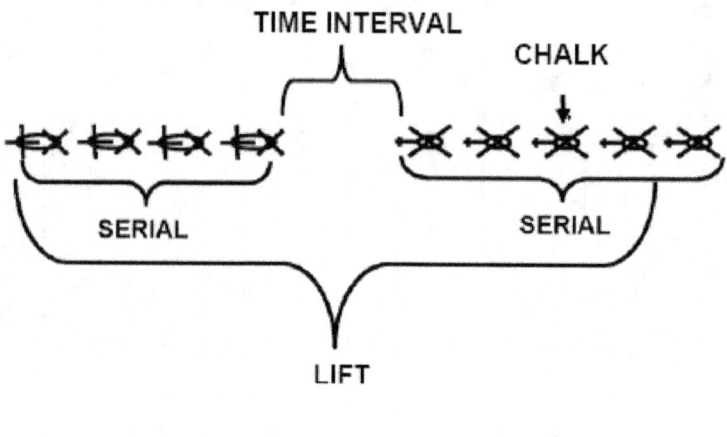

Purpose: The charts provide conversion for both standard and leap years.

Origin: BCTC Battle Staff Guide (AUG10)

Leap Year

Day	Jan	Feb	Mar	Apr	May	Jun	Jul	Aug	Sep	Oct	Nov	Dec
1	1	32	61	92	122	153	183	214	245	275	306	336
2	2	33	62	93	123	154	184	215	246	276	307	337
3	3	34	63	94	124	155	185	216	247	277	308	338
4	4	35	64	95	125	156	186	217	248	278	309	339
5	5	36	65	96	126	157	187	218	249	279	310	340
6	6	37	66	97	127	158	188	219	250	280	311	341
7	7	38	67	98	128	159	189	220	251	281	312	342
8	8	39	68	99	129	160	190	221	252	282	313	343
9	9	40	69	100	130	161	191	222	253	283	314	344
10	10	41	70	101	131	162	192	223	254	284	315	345
11	11	42	71	102	132	163	193	224	255	285	316	346
12	12	43	72	103	133	164	194	225	256	286	317	347
13	13	44	73	104	134	165	195	226	257	287	318	348
14	14	45	74	105	135	166	196	227	258	288	319	349
15	15	46	75	106	136	167	197	228	259	289	320	350
16	16	47	76	107	137	168	198	229	260	290	321	351
17	17	48	77	108	138	169	199	230	261	291	322	352
18	18	49	78	109	139	170	200	231	262	292	323	353
19	19	50	79	110	140	171	201	232	263	293	324	354
20	20	51	80	111	141	172	202	233	264	294	325	355
21	21	52	81	112	142	173	203	234	265	295	326	356
22	22	53	82	113	143	174	204	235	266	296	327	357
23	23	54	83	114	144	175	205	236	267	297	328	358
24	24	55	84	115	145	176	206	237	268	298	329	359
25	25	56	85	116	146	177	207	238	269	299	330	360
26	26	57	86	117	147	178	208	239	270	300	331	361
27	27	58	87	118	148	179	209	240	271	301	332	362
28	28	59	88	119	149	180	210	241	272	302	333	363
29	29	60	89	120	150	181	211	242	273	303	334	364
30	30		90	121	151	182	212	243	274	304	335	365
31	31		91		152		213	244		305		366

Non-Leap Year

Day	Jan	Feb	Mar	Apr	May	Jun	Jul	Aug	Sep	Oct	Nov	Dec
1	1	32	60	91	121	152	182	213	244	274	305	335
2	2	33	61	92	122	153	183	214	245	275	306	336
3	3	34	62	93	123	154	184	215	246	276	307	337
4	4	35	63	94	124	155	185	216	247	277	308	338
5	5	36	64	95	125	156	186	217	248	278	309	339
6	6	37	65	96	126	157	187	218	249	279	310	340
7	7	38	66	97	127	158	188	219	250	280	311	341
8	8	39	67	98	128	159	189	220	251	281	312	342
9	9	40	68	99	129	160	190	221	252	282	313	343
10	10	41	69	100	130	161	191	222	253	283	314	344
11	11	42	70	101	131	162	192	223	254	284	315	345
12	12	43	71	102	132	163	193	224	255	285	316	346
13	13	44	72	103	133	164	194	225	256	286	317	347
14	14	45	73	104	134	165	195	226	257	287	318	348
15	15	46	74	105	135	166	196	227	258	288	319	349
16	16	47	75	106	136	167	197	228	259	289	320	350
17	17	48	76	107	137	168	198	229	260	290	321	351
18	18	49	77	108	138	169	199	230	261	291	322	352
19	19	50	78	109	139	170	200	231	262	292	323	353
20	20	51	79	110	140	171	201	232	263	293	324	354
21	21	52	80	111	141	172	202	233	264	294	325	355
22	22	53	81	112	142	173	203	234	265	295	326	356
23	23	54	82	113	143	174	204	235	266	296	327	357
24	24	55	83	114	144	175	205	236	267	297	328	358
25	25	56	84	115	145	176	206	237	268	298	329	359
26	26	57	85	116	146	177	207	238	269	299	330	360
27	27	58	86	117	147	178	208	239	270	300	331	361
28	28	59	87	118	148	179	209	240	271	301	332	362
29	29		88	119	149	180	210	241	272	302	333	363
30	30		89	120	150	181	211	242	273	303	334	364
31	31		90		151		212	243		304		365

Conversion Factors

Purpose: The charts provide the metric to standard conversions.

Conversion Factors (Weight)

Unit of Measure	Long tons	Metric tons	Short tons	Kilograms	Pounds
1 long ton =		1.0160	1.1200	1,016.0	2,240.0
1 metric ton =	0.9842		1.1023	1,000.0	2,204.6
1 short ton =	0.8929	0.9072		907.2	2,000.0
1 kilogram =					2.2046

Conversion Factors (Speed)

Unit of Measure	Knots	Statute miles per hour	Kilo- meters per hour
1 knot =		1.1516	1.8532
1 mile per hour =	0.8684		1.6093
1 km per hour =	0.5396	0.6214	

Unit of Measure	Feet per minute	Feet per second	Meters per minute	Meters per second
1 knot =	101.34	1.6890	30.89	0.5148
1 mile per hour =	88.00	1.4667	26.82	0.4470
1 km per hour =	54.68	0.9113	16.67	0.2778

Unit of Measure	Nautical miles	Statute miles	Kilo- meters	Meters	Yards
1 nautical mile =		1.1516	1.8532	1,853.2	2,026.8
1 statute mile =	0.8684		1.6093	1,609.3	1,760.0
1 kilometer =	0.5396	0.6214		1,000	1,093.6
1 cable length =	0.1184	0.1364	0.2195	219.5	240.0
1 fathom =				1.829	2.0
1 meter =					1.0936
1 yard =				0.9144	
1 foot =				0.3048	0.3333
1 inch =					
1 centimeter =					

Chapter 2 – Detailed Planning

With abundant courses, schools, and processes, in both the civilian and military world, detailed planning is received with ominous reverence and fear.   When boiled to its individual components, detailed planning is simple. A problem is identified and its contributing factors and possible tools are gathered. Planning participants proceed to develop methods of overcoming the problem. These solutions are then weighed against each other and the preferred method is selected and given to others verbally or in a written product.

 This chapter outlines various military methods to conduct detailed planning but the simple outline does not change. If a step or example is found in military doctrine, the doctrinal reference is noted.

Military Decision Making Process (MDMP)

Reference: ATTP 5-0.1

Key inputs	Steps	Key outputs
• Higher headquarters' plan or order or a new mission anticipated by the commander	Step 1: **Receipt of Mission**	• Commander's initial guidance • Initial allocation of time
	Warning order	
• Higher headquarters' plan or order • Higher headquarters' knowledge and intelligence products • Knowledge products from other organizations • Design concept (if developed)	Step 2: **Mission Analysis**	• Problem statement • Mission statement • Initial commander's intent • Initial planning guidance • Initial CCIRs and EEFIs • Updated IPB and running estimates • Assumptions
	Warning order	

• Mission statement
• Initial commander's intent, planning guidance, CCIRs, and EEFIs
• Updated IPB and running estimates
• Assumptions
	Step 3:
	Course of Action (COA) Development
		• COA statements and sketches
		  - Tentative task organization
		  - Broad concept of operations
		• Revised planning guidance
		• Updated assumptions

• Updated running estimates • Revised planning guidance • COA statements and sketches • Updated assumptions	Step 4: **COA Analysis (War Game)**	• Refined COAs • Potential decision points • War-game results • Initial assessment measures • Updated assumptions
• Updated running estimates • Refined COAs • Evaluation criteria • War-game results • Updated assumptions	Step 5: **COA Comparison**	• Evaluated COAs • Recommended COAs • Updated running estimates • Updated assumptions
• Updated running estimates • Evaluated COAs • Recommended COA • Updated assumptions	Step 6: **COA Approval**	• Commander-selected COA and any modifications • Refined commander's intent, CCIRs, and EEFIs • Updated assumptions
	Warning order	
• Commander-selected COA with any modifications • Refined commander's intent, CCIRs, and EEFIs • Updated assumptions	Step 7: **Orders Production**	• Approved operation plan or order

Step 1 – Receipt of Mission

Inputs
•Higher HQ plan or order (ATTP 5-0.1)
•Higher HQ intelligence and knowledge products (ATTP 5-0.1)

Outputs
•Commander's initial guidance (ATTP 5-0.1)
•Initial time allocation (ATTP 5-0.1)
•WARNO 1
•Standardized map established
•Required orders and overlays inventoried
•Task organized planning team
•Staff estimate template
•Planning timeline

Step 2 – Mission Analysis

Inputs
- Higher HQ plan or order (ATTP 5-0.1)
- Higher HQ intelligence and knowledge products (ATTP 5-0.1)
- Updated running estimates (ATTP 5-0.1)
- Initial commander's guidance (ATTP 5-0.1)
- COA evaluation criteria (ATTP 5-0.1)
- Design concept (ATTP 5-0.1)
  - Problem Statement
  - Operational Approach
- Mission analysis brief template

Outputs
- Approved problem statement (ATTP 5-0.1)
- Approved mission statement (ATTP 5-0.1)
- Initial commander's intent (ATTP 5-0.1)
- Initial CCIRs and EEFIs (ATTP 5-0.1)
- Initial commander's planning guidance (ATTP 5-0.1)
- Information themes and messages (ATTP 5-0.1)
- Updated IPB products (ATTP 5-0.1)
- Updated running estimates (ATTP 5-0.1)
- Assumptions (ATTP 5-0.1)
- Resource shortfalls (ATTP 5-0.1)
- Updated operational timeline (ATTP 5-0.1)
- COA evaluation criteria (ATTP 5-0.1)
  - TTP: Glean from problem statement.
- WARNO 2 (ATTP 5-0.1)

Recommended Mission Analysis Briefing Agenda
- Title slide
- Purpose of the brief
- Agenda

- Initial planning guidance
- Situation Update
  - Problem statement
  - Higher HQ Mission and Intent
  - Inputs – Orders/CO Guidance/INSUMs
  - Current Friendly Disposition
  - Command Relationships (Nesting Diagram)
  - Task Organization (with as of dates for relationships)
  - Operational Timeline
  - Proposed AO/AI
- Intelligence Estimate
  - Terrain analysis (MCOO)
  - Weather analysis
  - Human environment estimate/cultural analysis
  - PMESII-PT Analysis
  - Enemy Analysis
    - DOCTEMP
    - SITEMP
    - Threat capabilities by WFF
    - Threat COAs
  - COG Analysis (optional)
- Friendly assessment
  - Specified/implied/essential tasks (include origin)
  - Facts
  - Assumptions
  - Limitations
  - Shortfalls (optional based on commander)
  - Deductions
  - Draft HPTL
  - Initial Collection Plan
  - Risk
  - Proposed CCIR (PIR, FFIR)
  - Proposed mission/intent
  - Proposed evaluation criteria

- Conclusion/recommendation
- Planning Timeline
- Hidden Slides
  - Warfighting Functions required by the mission
    - Medical
    - Bridging
    - Breaching
    - Others
  - Staff Estimates

Step 3 – COA Development

Inputs
- RCPA (Relative Combat Power Assessment) – numerical/narrative
- Wargame Synch Matrix Format
- Decision Support Matrix Format
- Approved problem statement (ATTP 5-0.1)
- Approved mission statement (ATTP 5-0.1)
- Initial commander's intent and planning guidance (ATTP 5-0.1)
- Design inputs (ATTP 5-0.1)
- Specified and implied tasks (ATTP 5-0.1)
- Assumptions (ATTP 5-0.1)
- Updated running estimates and IPB products (ATTP 5-0.1)
- Naming conventions
- Framework for the COAs (Deep/Close/Security, Decisive-Shaping-Sustaining, or Main and Supporting Efforts)
- COA development plan (parallel or sequential)

Outputs
- Decision Support Matrix (DSM)
- Updated Graphics
- Commander's selectd COAs for wargaming with COA statements and sketches (ATTP 5-0.1)
- Commander's refined planning guidance including wargaming guidance / evaluation criteria (ATTP 5-0.1)
- Updated running estimates and IPB products (ATTP 5-0.1)
- Updated assumptions (ATTP 5-0.1)
- Relative combat power: quantitative and qualitative
- Deception options

Recommended COA Development Brief Agenda
- Title slide

- Purpose of the brief
- Agenda
- Commander's planning guidance
- Operational Update
  - Problem statement
  - Higher HQ Mission and Intent
  - Inputs – Orders/CO Guidance/INSUMs
  - Mission and Commander's Intent
  - Current Friendly Disposition
  - Command Relationships (Nesting Diagram)
  - Task Organization
  - Proposed AO/AI
  - COA Neutral Assumptions
  - COG Analysis (optional)
  - Relative Combat Power Assessment
- Intelligence Update
  - Updated Terrain analysis (MCOO)
  - Updated Weather analysis
  - Updated Human environment estimate/cultural analysis
  - Updated PMESII-PT Analysis
  - Updated Enemy Analysis
    - DOCTEMP
    - SITEMP
    - Threat capabilities by WFF
    - Threat COAs
  - Proposed CCIR
  - Event Matrix
  - Proposed FFIR
- COAs (use similar template for each COA)
  - COA components
  - COA specific assumptions
  - COA statement
  - Task organization
  - COA steps/phases

- COA Risk
- Fires
- HPTL
- Sustainment
- Decision Support Matrix
- Relative Combat Power
- COA common concepts
  - Mission command (command and control)
  - Information operaitons
  - DC operations
  - EPW operations
  - Medical support
  - Collection plan
  - Deception options
- Recommended Wargame Guidance
- Questions
- Planning timeline

Intelligence Collection Plan (Example)

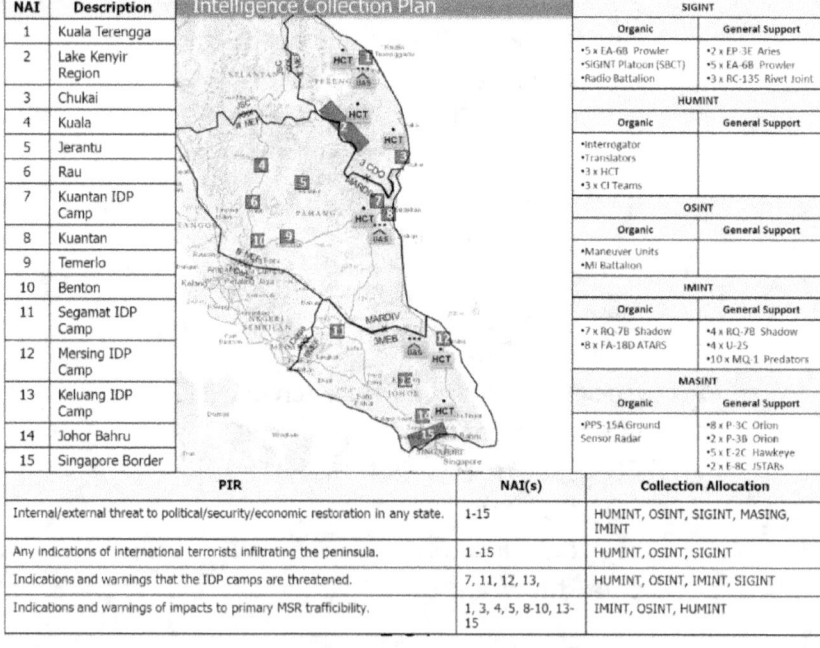

NAI	Description
1	Kuala Terengga
2	Lake Kenyir Region
3	Chukai
4	Kuala
5	Jerantu
6	Rau
7	Kuantan IDP Camp
8	Kuantan
9	Temerlo
10	Benton
11	Segamat IDP Camp
12	Mersing IDP Camp
13	Keluang IDP Camp
14	Johor Bahru
15	Singapore Border

SIGINT	
Organic	General Support
•5 x EA-6B Prowler	•2 x EP-3E Aries
•SIGINT Platoon (SBCT)	•5 x EA-6B Prowler
•Radio Battalion	•3 x RC-135 Rivet Joint

HUMINT	
Organic	General Support
•Interrogator	
•Translators	
•3 x HCT	
•3 x CI Teams	

OSINT	
Organic	General Support
•Maneuver Units	
•MI Battalion	

IMINT	
Organic	General Support
•7 x RQ-7B Shadow	•4 x RQ-7B Shadow
•8 x FA-18D ATARS	•4 x U-2S
	•10 x MQ 1 Predators

MASINT	
Organic	General Support
•PPS-15A Ground Sensor Radar	•8 x P-3C Orion
	•2 x P-3B Orion
	•5 x E-2C Hawkeye
	•2 x E-8C JSTARs

PIR	NAI(s)	Collection Allocation
Internal/external threat to political/security/economic restoration in any state.	1-15	HUMINT, OSINT, SIGINT, MASING, IMINT
Any indications of international terrorists infiltrating the peninsula.	1 -15	HUMINT, OSINT, SIGINT
Indications and warnings that the IDP camps are threatened.	7, 11, 12, 13,	HUMINT, OSINT, IMINT, SIGINT
Indications and warnings of impacts to primary MSR trafficability.	1, 3, 4, 5, 8-10, 13-15	IMINT, OSINT, HUMINT

COA Statement and Sketch

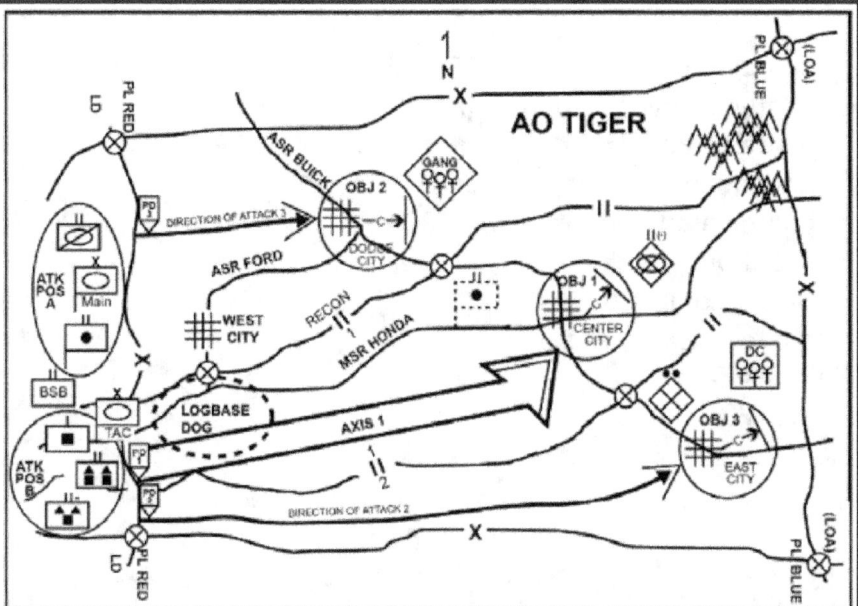

MISSION: On order, 3d HBCT clears remnants of the 72d Brigade in AO TIGER to establish security and enable the host-nation in reestablishing civil control and governance in the region.

INTENT: The purpose of this operation is to provide a safe and secure environment in AO TIGER that enables the host-nation and other civilian organization to reestablish civil control, restore essential services, and reestablish local governance within the area. At end state, the BCT has cleared remnant enemy forces in AO TIGER, secured population centers, and is prepared to transition responsibility for security to host-nation authority.

DECISIVE OPERATION: Combined Arms BN #1 (two armor/two mech) (ME) begins movement from ATK POS B, crosses LD at PD 1, and attacks along AXIS 1 to clear remnants of the 72d Brigade and secure the population in OBJ 1.

SHAPING OPERATIONS: Combined Arms BN #2 (-) (two armor/one mech) in the SOUTH follows Combined Arms BN #1 from ATK POS A, crosses LD at PD 2, and attacks along DIRECTION OF ATTACK 2 to clear OBJ 3 and provide security to dislocated civilian site vicinity EAST CITY. RECON squadron in the NORTH begins movement from ATK POS A, crosses LD at PD 3, and attacks along DIRECTION OF ATTACK 3 to clear hostile gang vic OBJ 2 and provide security to enable NGO delivery of humanitarian assistance to WEST CITY and DODGE CITY. 3rd HBCT Main CP moves and co-locates with RECON squadron.

The BCT reserve, Mech Company, locates with BSB vic AA DOG with priority of commitment: 1) OBJ 1 in support of Combined Arms BN #1; 2) MSR HONDA security; and 3) Security of supply/relief convoys.

3d HBCT TAC CP moves and co-locates with Combined Arms BN #1 in OBJ 1. HBCT main CP locates in ATK POS A. O/O moves and co-locates with RECON squadron in OBJ 2.

BCT FIRES will disrupt enemy mortars vic OBJ 1 and position to provide responsive precision fires to destroy remnant enemy forces in AO TIGER.

BCT RECONNAISSANCE AND SURVEILLANCE operations focus on: 1) Identifying the location and disposition of enemy forces vic. OBJ 1; 2) Observation of MSR HONDA between PL RED and PL BLUE; and 3) Observation of dislocated civilian traffic from CENTER CITY to EAST CITY.

SUSTAINING OPERATION: The BSB will establish LOGBASE DOG vic WEST CITY with MSR HONDA, ASR FORD, and ASR BUICK as the primary routes used to sustain operations. The BSB coordinates with humanitarian relief agencies to help rapidly restore essential services in AO TIGER.

TACTICAL RISK is assumed in the northeastern portion of AO TIGER by utilizing primarily reconnaissance and surveillance assets to maintain situational awareness of hostile elements that may use mountains to reconstitute forces.

AO	area of operations	HBCT	headquarters brigade combat team	OBJ	objective
ASR	alternate supply route	LC	line of contact	PD	point of departure
ATK POS	attack position	LD	line of departure	PL	phase line
BCT	brigade combat team	LOA	limit of advance	RECON	reconnaissance
BN	battalion	MECH	mechanized	TAC	tactical
BSB	brigade support battalion	MSR	main supply route	vic	vicinity
CP	command post	NGO	nongovernmental organization		
DC	displaced civilians	O/O	on order		

Step 4 – COA Analysis

Inputs

- Updated IPB products (ATTP 5-0.1)
- Updated running estimates (ATTP 5-0.1)
- Updated commander's planning guidance (ATTP 5-0.1)
- COA statements and sketches (ATTP 5-0.1)
- Updated assumptions (ATTP 5-0.1)
- Evaluation criteria
- Relative combat power analysis
- Updated task organization
- War game script
- Synch matrix
- COFM calculator

Outputs

- Refined COAs (ATTP 5-0.1)
- DSM and matrixes (ATTP 5-0.1)
- Synchronization matrixes (ATTP 5-0.1)
- Potential branches and sequels (ATTP 5-0.1)
- Updated running estimates (ATTP 5-0.1)
- Updated assumptions (ATTP 5-0.1)
- Wargaming brief (optional) (ATTP 5-0.1)

Additional Duties for War Gaming (Recommended)

- Arbitrator
- Recorder - Synch Matrix
- Parked Issue Board – identify items to be considered later
- Adjudication
- COFM Calculator
- Time Keeper
- Enemy/Friendly Attrition Monitor

Conduct of the Wargame (Recommended)

- Initial Disposition of Enemy Forces (Known) – Red Cell (6 minutes)
- Initial Disposition of Friendly Forces – COA Lead (6 minutes)
- Initial Population Status – Green Cell (6 minutes)
- Turn 1
  - Action – Blue – COA Lead (5 minutes)
  - Counteraction – Red – Red Cell (5 minutes)
  - Counteraction – Green – Green Cell (5 minutes)
  - BDA Assessment – G2 (4 minutes)
  - Step Analysis - COA Assistant Lead (10 minutes)
- Turn 2
  - Action – Blue – COA Lead (5 minutes)
  - Counteraction – Red – Red Cell (5 minutes)
  - Counteraction – Green – Green Cell (5 minutes)
  - BDA Assessment – G2 (4 minutes)
  - Step Analysis - COA Assistant Lead (10 minutes)
- Turn 3
  - Action – Blue – COA Lead (5 minutes)
  - Counteraction – Red – Red Cell (5 minutes)
  - Counteraction – Green – Green Cell (5 minutes)
  - Reaction – Blue – COA Lead (5 minutes)
  - BDA Assessment – G2 (4 minutes)
  - Step Analysis - COA Assistant Lead (10 minutes)

Recommended War Game Brief Agenda (Optional Brief)

- Title slide
- Purpose of the brief
- Agenda
- Commander's war game guidance
- Evaluation criteria
- Operational Update
  - Task organization
  - Higher HQ mission and intent
  - Mission and commander's intent

- AO/AI
- COA neutral assumptions
- COA Analysis (optional)
- Relative combat power assessment
- Intelligence update
  - Updated weather
  - Enemy COAs
  - Due outs from previous briefing
  - HVTs
  - Initial collection plan
- COAs (identical slides for each COA wargamed)
  - Findings BLUF (method used, FAS results)
  - COA summary (sketch/narrative)
  - COA task organization
  - Step/box wargamed
  - Time/phase analysis
  - COA fires
  - HPTL
  - Concept of support
  - Decision support matrix
  - Proposed COA changes
  - COA assumptions
  - Updated branches/sequels
  - CCIR
  - COA advantages/disadvantages
  - COA evaluation criteria
- Recommendations
  - Timeline comparison
  - Updated branches/sequels
- Comments/guidance
- Planning timeline

Wargaming Methods

Belt Method

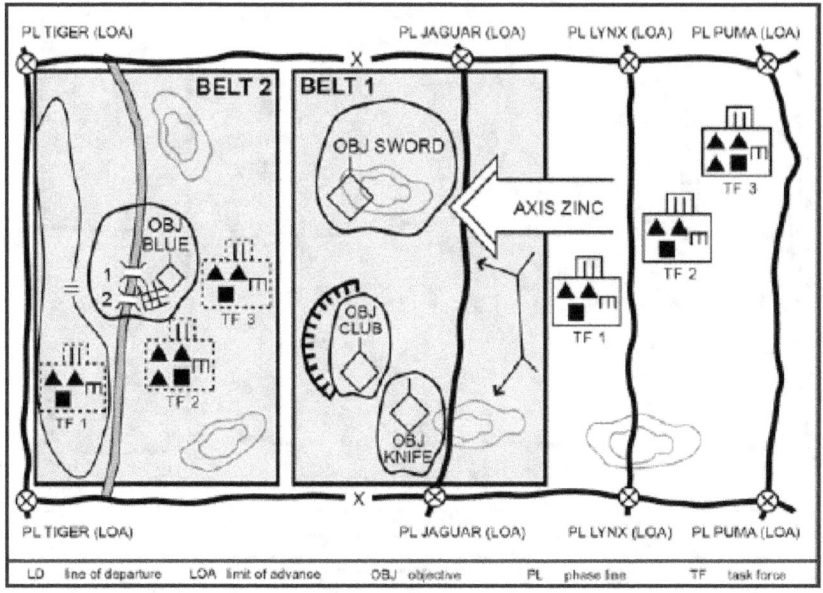

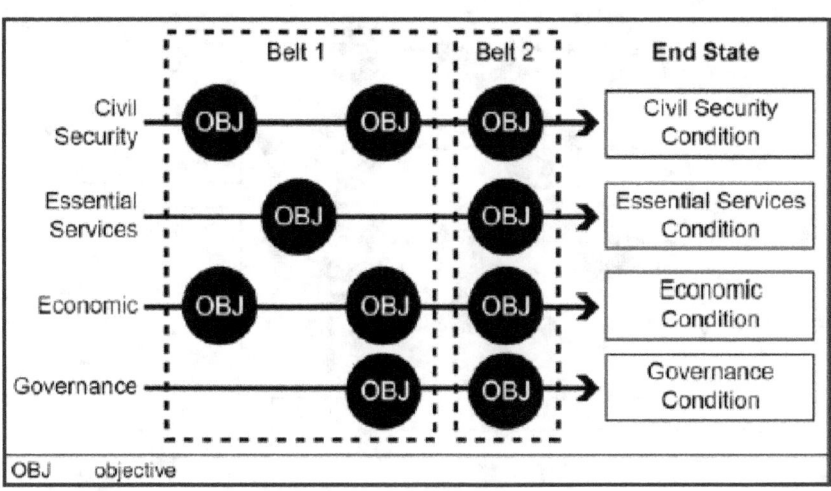

Avenue in Depth Method

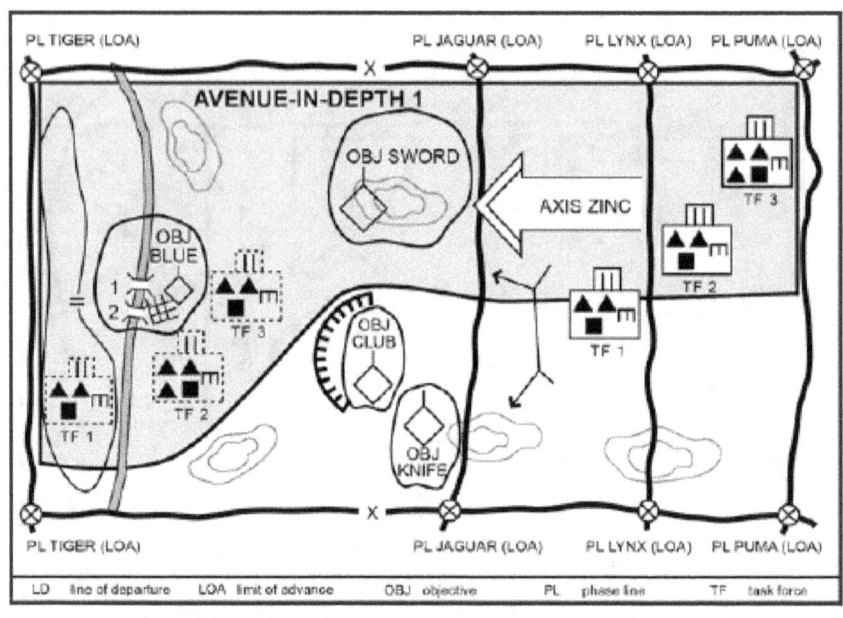

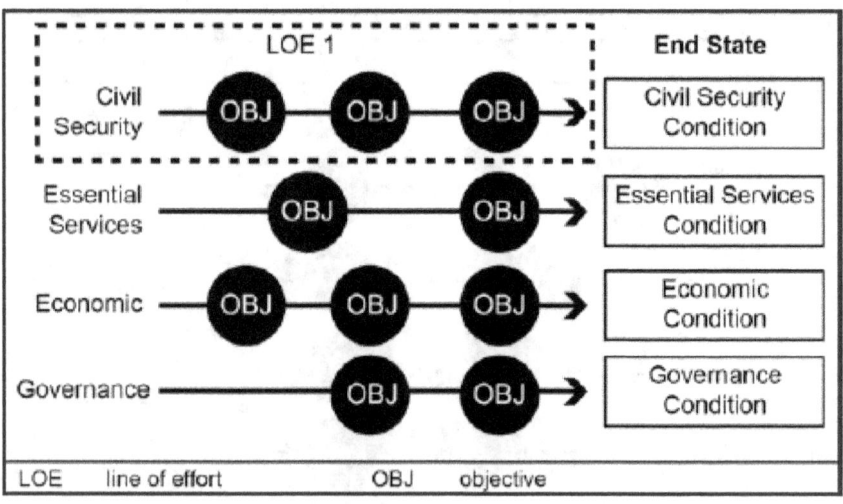

Box Method

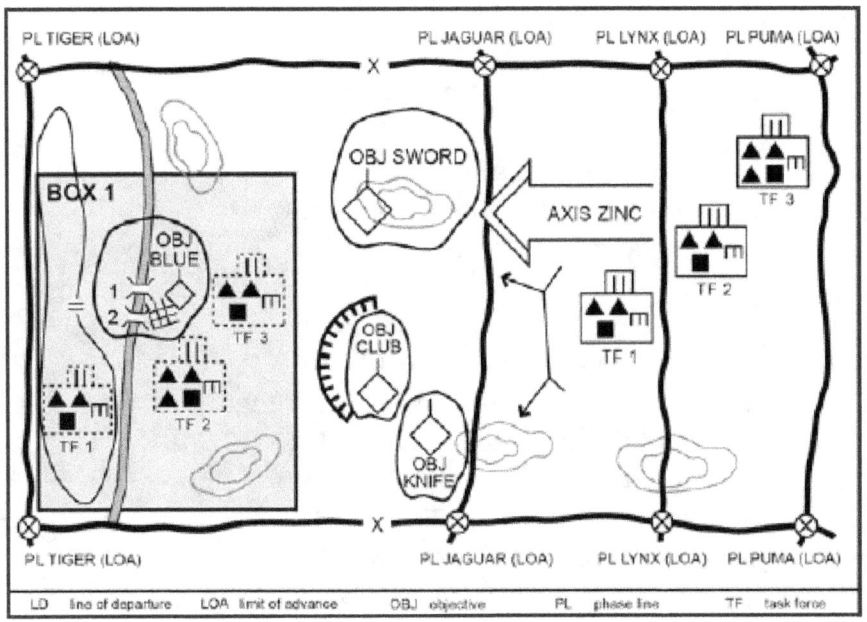

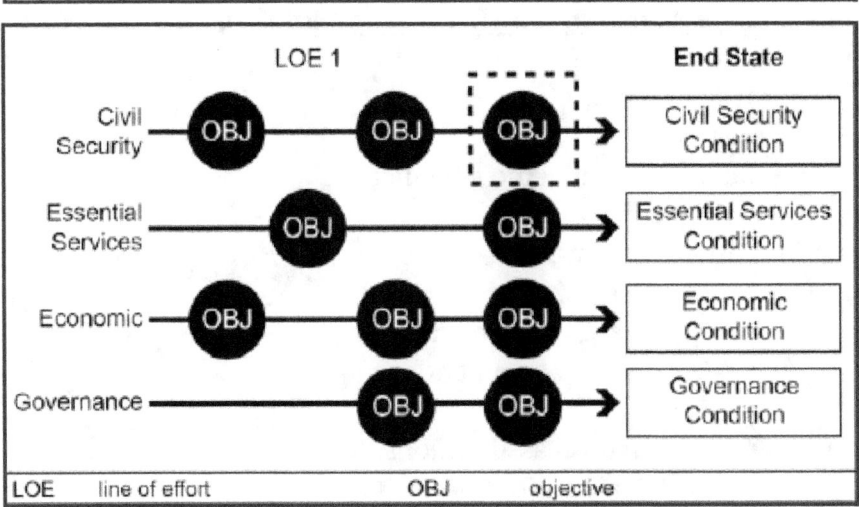

CALL Staff Officer's Quick Reference Guide (2013)

Step 5 – COA Comparison

Inputs
- War game results (ATTP 5-0.1)
- Evaluation criteria (ATTP 5-0.1)
- Updated running estimates (ATTP 5-0.1)
- Updated assumptions (ATTP 5-0.1)

Outputs
- Evaluated courses of action (ATTP 5-0.1)
- Recommended course of action (ATTP 5-0.1)
- Course of action selection rationale (ATTP 5-0.1)
- Updated running estimates (ATTP 5-0.1)
- Updated assumptions (ATTP 5-0.1)
- Course of action decision brief (ATTP 5-0.1)

Recommended COA Decision Brief Agenda*
- Title slide
- Purpose of the brief
- Agenda
- Commander's war game guidance
- Evaluation criteria
- Operational Update
  - Task organization
  - Higher HQ mission and intent
  - Mission and commander's intent
  - AO/AI
  - COA neutral assumptions
  - COA Analysis (optional)
  - Relative combat power assessment
- Intelligence update
  - Updated weather
  - Enemy COAs
  - Due outs from previous briefing

- HVTs
- Initial collection plan
- COAs (identical slides for each COA war gamed)
  - Findings BLUF (method used, FAS results)
  - COA summary (sketch/narrative)
  - COA task organization
  - Step/box war gamed
  - Time/phase analysis
  - COA fires
  - HPTL
  - Concept of support
  - Decision support matrix
  - Proposed COA changes
  - COA assumptions
  - Updated branches/sequels
  - CCIR
  - COA advantages/disadvantages
  - COA evaluation criteria
- Comparison
  - Criteria comparison
  - Required branch/sequel comparison
  - Timeline comparison
  - Narrative comparison
  - Decision Matrix (DECMAT)
- Recommendations
- Comments/guidance
- Planning timeline

*If the optional war game brief was conducted, the OPT should minimize redundancy within the presentation.

Step 6 – COA Approval

Inputs
•Evaluated COAs (ATTP 5-0.1)
•Recommended COAs (ATTP 5-0.1)
•Updated running estimates (ATTP 5-0.1)
•Updated assumptions (ATTP 5-0.1)

Outputs
•Approved COA (ATTP 5-0.1)
•Refined commander's intent (ATTP 5-0.1)
•Refined CCIR (ATTP 5-0.1)
•Refined EEFI (ATTP 5-0.1)
•Updated Assumptions (ATTP 5-0.1)
•WARNO 3 (ATTP 5-0.1)

Step 7 – Orders Production

Inputs
•Approved COA (ATTP 5-0.1)
•Refined Commander's Intent (ATTP 5-0.1)
•CCIR (ATTP 5-0.1)
•EEFI (ATTP 5-0.1)
•Updated assumptions (ATTP 5-0.1)

Outputs
•Approved OPORD (ATTP 5-0.1)

Annexes

ANNEX A – TASK ORGANIZATION (G-5 or G-3 [S-3])

ANNEX B – INTELLIGENCE (G-2 [S-2])

Appendix 1 – Intelligence Estimate
    Tab A – Terrain (Engineer Officer)
    Tab B – Weather (Staff Weather Officer)
    Tab C – Civil Considerations
    Tab D – Intelligence Preparation of the Battlefield Products
Appendix 2 – Counterintelligence
Appendix 3 – Signals Intelligence
Appendix 4 – Human Intelligence
Appendix 5 – Geospatial Intelligence
Appendix 6 – Measurement and Signature Intelligence
Appendix 7 – Open Source Intelligence

ANNEX C – OPERATIONS (G-5 or G-3 [S-3])

Appendix 1 – Design Concept
Appendix 2 – Operation Overlay
Appendix 3 – Decision Support Products
    Tab A – Execution Matrix
    Tab B – Decision Support Template and Matrix
Appendix 4 – Gap Crossing Operations
    Tab A – Traffic Control Overlay
Appendix 5 – Air Assault Operations
    Tab A – Pickup Zone Diagram
    Tab B – Air Movement Table
    Tab C – Landing Zone Diagram
Appendix 6 – Airborne Operations
    Tab A – Marshalling Plan
    Tab B – Air Movement Plan
    Tab C – Drop Zone/Extraction Zone Diagram
Appendix 7 – Amphibious Operations
    Tab A – Advance Force Operations
    Tab B – Embarkation Plan
    Tab C – Landing Plan
    Tab D – Rehearsal Plan
Appendix 8 – Special Operations (G-3 [S-3])
Appendix 9 – Battlefield Obscuration (CBRN Officer)
Appendix 10 – Airspace Command and Control (G-3 [S-3] or Airspace Command and Control Officer)
    Tab A – Air Traffic Services
Appendix 11 – Rules of Engagement (Staff Judge Advocate)
    Tab A – No Strike List
    Tab B – Restricted Target List (G-3 [S-3] with Staff Judge Advocate)
Appendix 12 – Law and Order Operations (Provost Marshal)
    Tab A – Police Engagement
    Tab B – Law Enforcement
Appendix 13 – Internment and Resettlement Operations (Provost Marshal)

ANNEX D – FIRES (Chief of Fires/Fire Support Officer)

Appendix 1 – Fire Support Overlay
Appendix 2 – Fire Support Execution Matrix
Appendix 3 – Targeting
  Tab A – Target Selection Standards
  Tab B – Target Synchronization Matrix
  Tab C – Attack Guidance Matrix
  Tab D – Target List Worksheets
  Tab E – Battle Damage Assessment (G-2 [S-2])
Appendix 4 – Field Artillery Support
Appendix 5 – Air Support
Appendix 6 – Naval Fire Support
Appendix 7 – Cyber/Electromagnetic Activities (Electronic Warfare Officer)
  Tab A – Electronic Warfare
  Tab B – Computer Network Operations
  Tab C – Computer Network Attack
  Tab D – Computer Network Exploitation

ANNEX E – PROTECTION (Chief of Protection/Protection Officer as designated by the commander)

Appendix 1 – Air and Missile Defense (Air and Missile Defense Officer)
  Tab A – Enemy Air Avenues of Approach
  Tab B – Enemy Air Order of Battle
  Tab C – Enemy Theater Ballistic Missile Overlay
  Tab D – Air and Missile Defense Protection Overlay
  Tab E – Critical Asset List/Defended Asset List
Appendix 2 – Personnel Recovery (Personnel Recovery Officer)
Appendix 3 – Fratricide Avoidance (Safety Officer)
Appendix 4 – Operational Area Security (Provost Marshal)
Appendix 5 – Antiterrorism (Antiterrorism Officer)
Appendix 6 – Chemical, Biological, Radiological, and Nuclear Defense (CBRN Officer)
Appendix 7 – Safety (Safety Officer)
Appendix 8 – Operations Security (Operations Security Officer)
Appendix 9 – Explosive Ordnance Disposal (Explosive Ordnance Disposal Officer)
Appendix 10 – Force Health Protection (Surgeon)

ANNEX F – SUSTAINMENT (Chief of Sustainment [S-4])

    Appendix 1 – Logistics (G-4 [S-4])
        Tab A – Sustainment Overlay
        Tab B – Maintenance
        Tab C – Transportation
            Exhibit 1 – Traffic Circulation and Control (Provost Marshal)
            Exhibit 2 – Traffic Circulation Overlay
            Exhibit 3 – Road Movement Table
            Exhibit 4 – Highway Regulation (Provost Marshal)
        Tab D – Supply
        Tab E – Field Services
        Tab F – Distribution
        Tab G – Contract Support Integration
        Tab H – Mortuary Affairs
        Tab I – Internment and Resettlement Support
    Appendix 2 – Personnel Services Support (G-1 [S-1])
        Tab A – Human Resources Support (G-1 [S-1])
        Tab B – Financial Management (G-8)
        Tab C – Legal Support (Staff Judge Advocate)
        Tab D – Religious Support (Chaplain)
        Tab E – Band Operations (G-1 [S-1])
    Appendix 3 – Army Heath System Support (Surgeon)

ANNEX G – ENGINEER (Engineer Officer)

    Appendix 1 – Mobility/Countermobility
        Tab A – Obstacle Overlay
    Appendix 2 – Survivability (Engineer Officer)
    Appendix 3 – General Engineering
    Appendix 4 – Geospatial Engineering
    Appendix 5 – Environmental Considerations
        Tab A – Environmental Assessments
        Tab B – Environmental Assessment Exemptions
        Tab C – Environmental Baseline Survey

ANNEX H – SIGNAL (G-6 [S-6])

    Appendix 1 – Information Assurance
    Appendix 2 – Voice and Data Network Diagrams
    Appendix 3 – Satellite Communications
    Appendix 4 – Foreign Data Exchanges
    Appendix 5 – Electromagnetic Spectrum Operations

ANNEX I – Not Used

ANNEX J – INFORM AND INFLUENCE ACTIVITIES (G-7 [S-7])

    Appendix 1 – Public Affairs (Public Affairs Officer)
    Appendix 2 – Military Deception (Military Deception Officer)
    Appendix 3 – Military Information Support Operations (Military Information Support Officer)
    Appendix 4 – Soldier and Leader Engagement

ANNEX K – CIVIL AFFAIRS OPERATIONS (G-9 [S-9])
Appendix 1 – Execution Matrix
Appendix 2 – Populace and Resources Control Plan
Appendix 3 – Civil Information Management Plan
ANNEX L – RECONNAISSANCE AND SURVEILLANCE (G-3 [S-3])
Appendix 1 – Reconnaissance and Surveillance Overlay
Appendix 2 – Reconnaissance and Surveillance Tasking Matrix
ANNEX M – ASSESSMENT (G-5 [S-5] or G-3 [S-3])
Appendix 1 – Nesting of Assessment Efforts
Appendix 2 – Assessment Framework
Appendix 3 – Assessment Working Group
ANNEX N – SPACE OPERATIONS (Space Operations Officer)
ANNEX O – Not Used
ANNEX P – HOST-NATION SUPPORT (G-4 [S-4])
ANNEX Q – Spare
ANNEX R – REPORTS (G-3 [S-3], G-5 [S-5], G-7, and Knowledge Management Officer)
ANNEX S – SPECIAL TECHNICAL OPERATIONS (Special Technical Operations Officer)
Appendix 1 – Special Technical Operations Capabilities Integration Matrix
Appendix 2 – Functional Area I Program and Objectives
Appendix 3 – Functional Area II Program and Objectives
ANNEX T – Spare
ANNEX U – INSPECTOR GENERAL (Inspector General)
ANNEX V – INTERAGENCY COORDINATION (G-3 [S-3] and G-9 [S-9])
ANNEX W – Spare
ANNEX X – Spare
ANNEX Y – Spare
ANNEX Z – DISTRIBUTION (G-3 [S-3] and Knowledge Management Officer)

ATTP 5-0.1 (SEP11)

Joint Planning

Joint Operation Planning Process (JOPP)	Military Decision Making Process (MDMP)	Marine Corps Planning Process (MCPP)	Navy Planning Process (NPP)
Initiation	Receipt of Mission		
Mission Analysis	Mission Analysis	Problem Framing	Mission Analysis
COA Development	COA Development	COA Development	COA Development
COA Analysis	COA Analysis	COA War Gaming	COA Analysis
COA Comparison	COA Comparison	COA Comparison & Decision	COA Comparison and Decision
COA Approval	COA Approval		
Orders Development	Orders Production	Orders Development	Plans and Orders Production
		Transition	Transition

OPT Work Plan

	27 OCT	28 OCT	29 OCT	1 NOV	2 NOV	3 NOV	4 NOV	5 NOV	8 NOV	9 NOV
Focus	Plan to Plan	Research	Environment & problem	DRAFT IPR#1	REFINE IPR#1	Rehearse Start Op Approach	Initial Operational Approach	Refine & Rehearse	Final Operational Approach	Refine & Rehearse
Inputs	Plan Directive	WG Guidance	Initial Perspectives	ES & PS Design Sketch	ES & PS Sketch/ Op. Considerations	IPR #1 CDR guidance	Approach Design Sketch	IPR#2 CDR Guidance	Refined Concept COS Guidance	IPR #3
Milestone				COS Desk Side		IPR#1	COS Desk Side	IPR#2	COS Desk Side	IPR#0
Activity	Work Plan	Initial Perspectives	Synthesize Perspectives	Running estimates/ COS Guidance	Eval criteria Initial CDR's intent Presentation Slides Rehearse IPR #1	Refine: ES & PS Running estimates Proposed CCIR	Integrate Guidance Production Sketch Virtual Walkthrough I	Integrate Guidance Reframe ES/PS & estimates (?)	Integrate Guidance Presentation Products Virtual Walkthrough II	
Output			ES & PS Design Sketch	ES & PS Production Sketch Operational Considerations	IPR#1 Brief	Approach Design Sketch	IPR#2 Brief	Refined Operational Concept	IPR#3 Brief	Approved design for NSC

WG Reorg: By Perspective Define Environments	WG Reorg: Consolidated Perspectives Frame Problem	WG Reorg: Staff Perspectives Conduct esitmates; competing operational hypothesis/considerations (US and Mexican perspectives)	WG Reorganization Develop competing approaches	WG Reorg; staff proponents to develop operational details

IPRs with CG

IPR #1: 031100 – 031300 NOV 10
Purpose:
1. CG decision to approve problem statement
2. CG guidance for operational approach
Discussion:
1. Environmental statement and sketch
2. Problem statement and sketch
3. Operational considerations

IPR #2: 051230– 05133000 NOV 10
Purpose:
1. CG decision to approve operational approach
2. CG guidance for refinement
Discussion:
1. Operational approach narrative and sketch

IPR #3: 091230– 09133000 NOV 10
Purpose:
1. CG decision to approve conceptual plan
2. CG decision to approve products for SECDEF
Discussion:
1. Environmental context
2. Problem statement
3. Operational approach narrative and sketch
4. Initial intent
5. Initial planning guidance
6. Email and information paper to SECDEF

Joint Operation Planning Activities, Functions, and Products

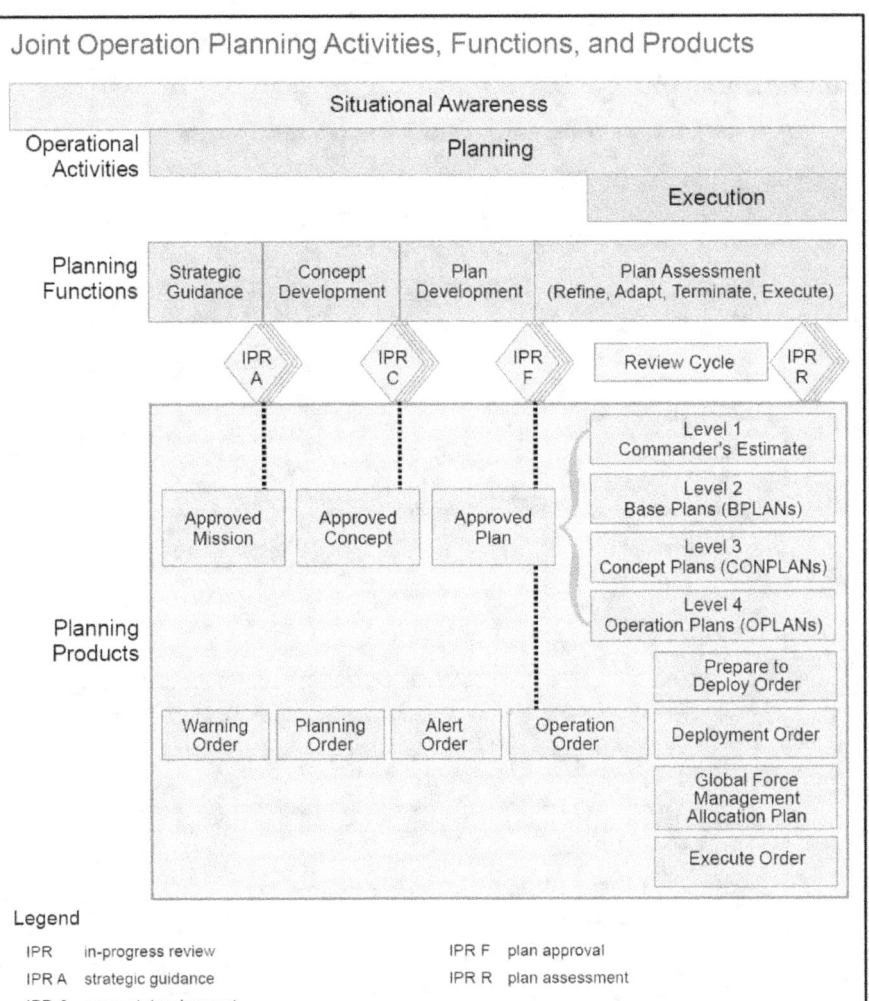

	Situational Awareness			
Operational Activities	Planning			
			Execution	

Planning Functions	Strategic Guidance	Concept Development	Plan Development	Plan Assessment (Refine, Adapt, Terminate, Execute)

IPR A   IPR C   IPR F   Review Cycle   IPR R

Planning Products

- Approved Mission
- Approved Concept
- Approved Plan

- Level 1 — Commander's Estimate
- Level 2 — Base Plans (BPLANs)
- Level 3 — Concept Plans (CONPLANs)
- Level 4 — Operation Plans (OPLANs)

- Warning Order
- Planning Order
- Alert Order
- Operation Order
- Prepare to Deploy Order
- Deployment Order
- Global Force Management Allocation Plan
- Execute Order

Legend

IPR   in-progress review   IPR F   plan approval

IPR A   strategic guidance   IPR R   plan assessment

IPR C   concept development

Step 2 – Mission Analysis

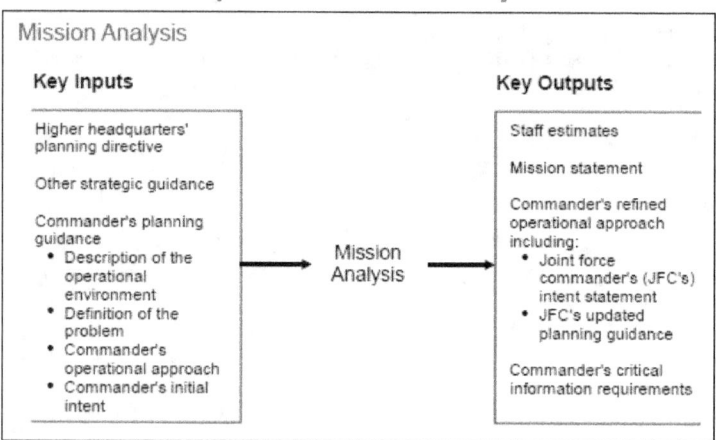

Mission Analysis

Key Inputs

Higher headquarters' planning directive

Other strategic guidance

Commander's planning guidance
- Description of the operational environment
- Definition of the problem
- Commander's operational approach
- Commander's initial intent

Mission Analysis

Key Outputs

Staff estimates

Mission statement

Commander's refined operational approach including:
- Joint force commander's (JFC's) intent statement
- JFC's updated planning guidance

Commander's critical information requirements

Mission Analysis Activities

- Analyze higher headquarters planning activities and strategic guidance
- Review commander's initial planning guidance, including his initial understanding of the operational environment, of the problem, and description of the operational approach
- Determine known facts and develop planning assumptions
- Determine and analyze operational limitations
- Determine specified, implied, and essential tasks
- Develop mission statement
- Conduct initial force allocation review
- Develop risk assesment
- Develop mission success criteria
- Develop commander's critical information requirements
- Prepare staff estimates
- Prepare and deliver mission analysis brief
- Publish commander's updated planning guidance, intent statement, and refined operational approach

Steps are not necessarily sequential.

Example Mission Analysis Briefing

- Introduction
- Situation overview
  - Operational environment (including joint operations area) and threat overview
  - Political, military, economic, social, information, and infrastructure strengths and weaknesses
  - Red threat (including center of gravity)
- Friendly assessment
  - Facts and assumptions
  - Limitations—constraints/restraints
  - Capabilities allocated
  - Legal considerations
- Communications strategy
- Objectives, effects, and task analysis
  - United States Government interagency objectives
  - Higher commander's objectives/mission/guidance
  - Objectives and effects
  - Specified/implied/essential tasks
  - Centers of gravity
- Operational protection
  - Operational risk
  - Mitigation
- Proposed initial commander's critical information requirements
- Mission
  - Proposed mission statement
  - Proposed commander's intent
- Command relationships
- Conclusion—potential resource shortfalls
- Mission analysis approval and commander's course of action planning guidance

Step 3 – COA Development

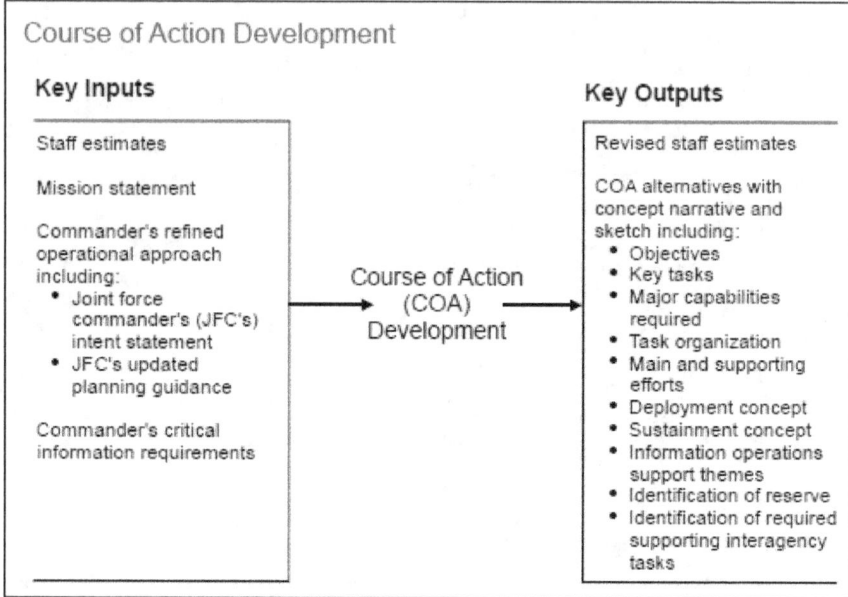

Course of Action Development

Key Inputs

Staff estimates

Mission statement

Commander's refined
operational approach
including:
* Joint force
  commander's (JFC's)
  intent statement
* JFC's updated
  planning guidance

Commander's critical
information requirements

Course of Action
(COA)
Development

Key Outputs

Revised staff estimates

COA alternatives with
concept narrative and
sketch including:
* Objectives
* Key tasks
* Major capabilities
  required
* Task organization
* Main and supporting
  efforts
* Deployment concept
* Sustainment concept
* Information operations
  support themes
* Identification of reserve
* Identification of required
  supporting interagency
  tasks

Step-by-Step Approach to Course of Action Development

Step   Action

1   Determine how much force will be needed in the theater at the end of the campaign, what those forces will be doing, and how those forces will be postured geographically. Use troop-to-task analysis. Draw a sketch to help visualize the forces and their locations.

2   Looking at the sketch and working backwards, determine the best way to get the forces postured in Step 1 from their ultimate positions at the end of the campaign to a base in friendly territory. This will help formulate the desired basing plan.

3   Using the mission statement as a guide, determine the tasks the force must accomplish en route to their locations/positions at the end of the campaign. Draw a sketch of the maneuver plan. Make sure the force does everything the Secretary of Defense (SecDef) has directed the commander to do (refer to specified tasks from the mission analysis).

4   Determine the basing required to posture the force in friendly territory, and the tasks the force must accomplish to get to those bases. Sketch this as part of the deployment plan.

5   Determine if the planned force is enough to accomplish all the tasks SecDef has given the commander. Adjust the force strength to fit the tasks. This should provide the answer to the first question.

6   Given the tasks to be performed, determine in what order the forces should be deployed into theater. Consider the force categories such as combat, protection, sustainment, theater enablers, and theater opening. This should answer the second question.

7   The information developed should now answer the remaining questions regarding force employment, major tasks and their sequencing, sustainment, and command relationships.

Example Course of Action Development Briefing

- Operations Directorate of a Joint Staff (J-3)/Plans Directorate of a Joint Staff (J-5)
  - Context/background (i.e., road to war)
  - Initiation—review guidance for initiation
  - Strategic guidance—planning tasks assigned to supported commander, forces/resources apportioned, planning guidance, updates, defense agreements, theater campaign plan(s), Guidance for Employment of the Force/Joint Strategic Capabilities Plan
  - Forces apportioned/assigned

- Intelligence Directorate of a Joint Staff (J-2)
  - Joint Intelligence Preparation of the Operational Environment
  - Enemy courses of action (COAs)—most dangerous, most likely; strengths and weaknesses

- J-3/J-5
  - Update facts and assumptions
  - Mission statement
  - Commander's intent (purpose, method, end state)
  - End state: political/military
    - termination criteria
  - Center of gravity analysis results: critical factors; strategic/operational
  - Joint operations area/theater of operations/communications zone sketch
  - Phase 0 shaping activities recommended (for current theater campaign plan)
  - Flexible deterrent options with desired effect
  - For each COA, sketch and statement by phase
    - task organization
    - component tasking
    - timeline
    - recommended command and control by phase
    - lines of operation/lines of effort
    - logistics estimates and feasibility
    - COA risks
  - COA summarized distinctions
  - COA priority for analysis

- Commander's Guidance

Step 4 – COA Analysis and War Gaming

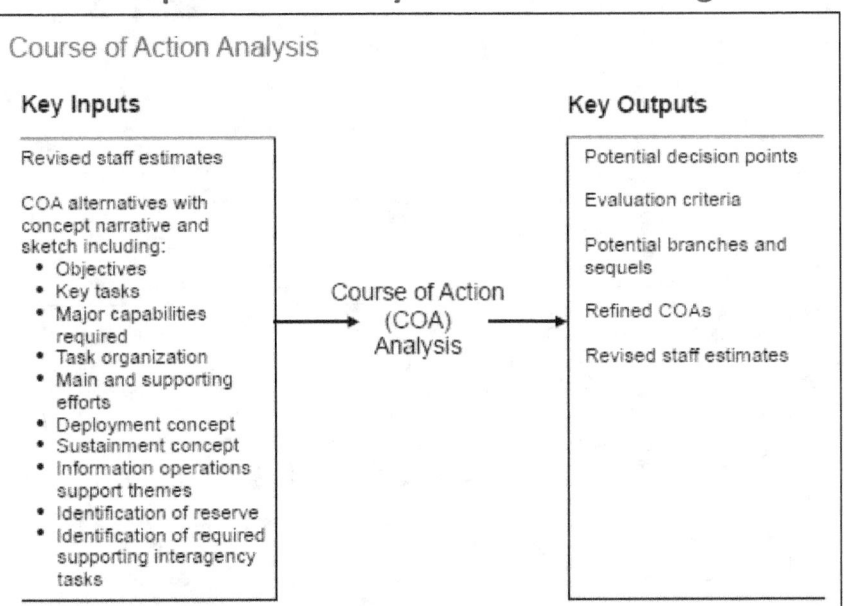

Course of Action Analysis

Key Inputs

Revised staff estimates

COA alternatives with concept narrative and sketch including:
- Objectives
- Key tasks
- Major capabilities required
- Task organization
- Main and supporting efforts
- Deployment concept
- Sustainment concept
- Information operations support themes
- Identification of reserve
- Identification of required supporting interagency tasks

Course of Action (COA) Analysis

Key Outputs

Potential decision points

Evaluation criteria

Potential branches and sequels

Refined COAs

Revised staff estimates

Step 5 – COA Comparison

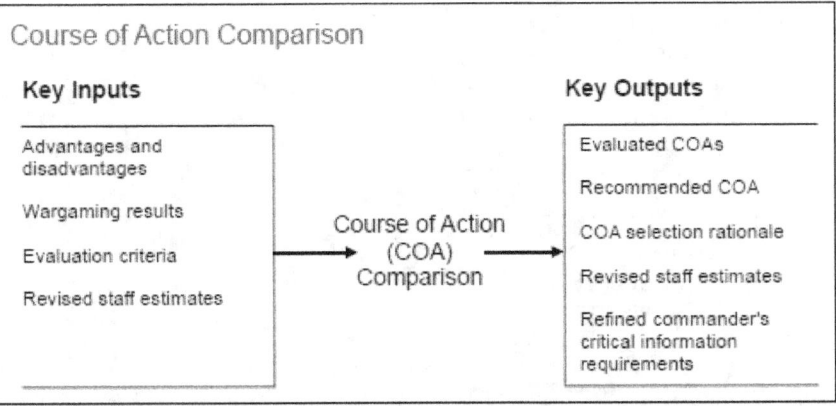

Course of Action Comparison

Key Inputs

Advantages and disadvantages

Wargaming results

Evaluation criteria

Revised staff estimates

Course of Action (COA) Comparison

Key Outputs

Evaluated COAs

Recommended COA

COA selection rationale

Revised staff estimates

Refined commander's critical information requirements

Step 6 – COA Approval

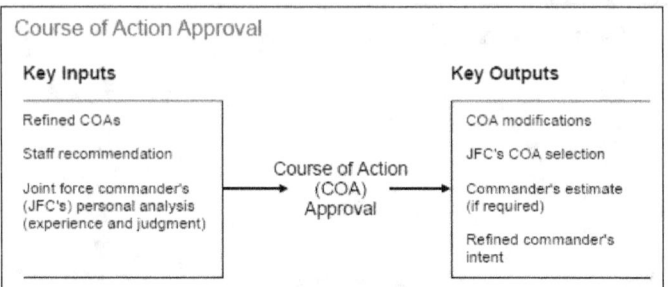

Course of Action Approval

Key Inputs

Refined COAs

Staff recommendation

Joint force commander's
(JFC's) personal analysis
(experience and judgment)

→ Course of Action
(COA)
Approval →

Key Outputs

COA modifications

JFC's COA selection

Commander's estimate
(if required)

Refined commander's
intent

Sample Course of Action Briefing Guide

- Purpose of the briefing
- Opposing situation
  - **Strength.** A review of opposing forces, both committed and available for reinforcement
  - **Composition.** Order of battle, major weapons systems, and operational characteristics
  - **Location and disposition.** Ground combat and fire support forces; air, naval, and missile forces; logistics forces and nodes; command and control facilities; and other combat power
  - **Reinforcements.** Land; air; naval; missile; chemical, biological, radiological, and nuclear; other advanced weapons systems; capacity for movement of these forces
  - **Logistics** Summary of opposing forces ability to support combat operations
  - **Time and space factors.** The capacity to move and reinforce positions
  - **Combat efficiency.** The state of training, readiness, battle experience, physical condition, morale, leadership, motivation, tactical doctrine, discipline, and significant strengths and weaknesses
- Friendly situation (similar elements as opposing situation)
- Mission statements
- Commander's intent statement
- Operational concepts and courses of action (COAs)
  - Any changes from the mission analysis briefing in the following areas:
    – assumptions
    – limitations
    – adversary and friendly centers of gravity (COGs)
    – phasing of the operation (if phased)
    – lines of operation/lines of effort
  - Present courses of action. As a minimum, discuss:
    – COA# _____ (short name, e.g., "Simultaneous Assault")
    – COA statement (brief concept of operations)
    – COA sketch
    – COA architecture
      - task organization
      - command relationships
      - organization of the operational area
    – major differences between each COA
    – summaries of COAs
  - COA analysis
    – review of the joint planning group's wargaming efforts
    – add considerations from own experiences
  - COA comparisons
    – description of comparison criteria (e.g., evaluation criteria) and comparison methodology
    – weigh strengths and weaknesses with respect to comparison criteria
  - COA recommendations
    – staff
    – components

Step 7 – Plan or Order Development

Plan Development Activities

- Force planning
- Support planning
- Nuclear strike planning
- Deployment and redeployment planning
- Shortfall identification

- Feasibility analysis
- Refinement
- Documentation
- Plan review and approval
- Supporting plan development

Chapter 3 - Conceptual Planning

The term "design" when linked to planning yields multiple emotional outcomes to include delight, fear, confusion, and hatred. At its core, design is a method of gaining an understanding of a problem to help develop a broad operational approach. The origin of design desired a method of understanding, unencumbered by a systematic planning process. Unfortunately, some past planners felt that they could conduct design, develop a very broad situational understanding, and they were complete with the process. Adequate design does not replace the need for detailed precise plans at its conclusion.

This chapter provides a brief description of several military design methods. There remains controversy over the rigidity of the processes but they are currently in use at the different echelons.

Army Design Methodology

Reference: ADRP 5-0 (MAY12)

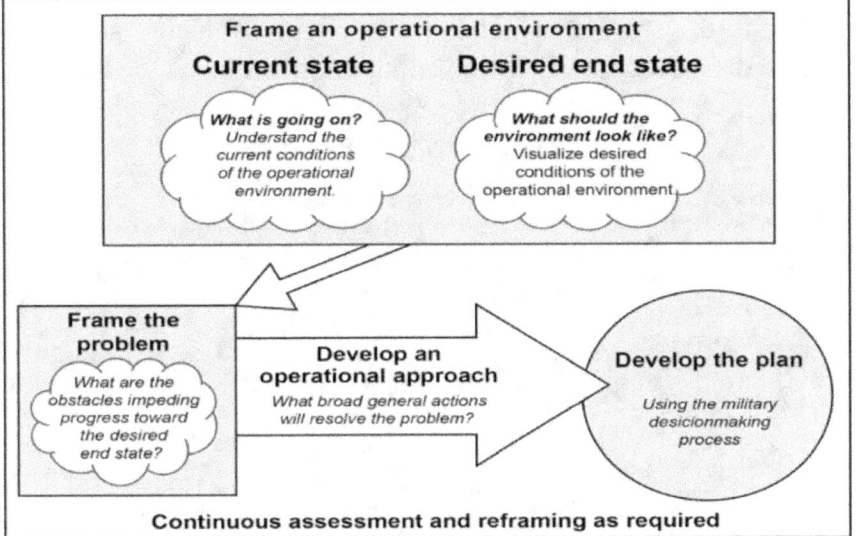

Outputs

- Problem Statement (ADRP 5-0)
- Initial Commander's Intent (ADRP 5-0)
    - Expanded Purpose
    - Key Tasks
    - Endstate
- Planning Guidance (ADRP 5-0)
    - Visualization
    - Description of the Operational Approach
    - Explain When/Where/How of Combat Power
    - Nesting with Commander's Intent
- Operational Environment/Problem Framing Brief (optional)
- Operational Approach brief (optional)

Framing the Operational Environment

- To frame the operational environment, utilize multiple models to enable an understanding of the current state.
- The future state is framed in terms of current higher guidance and directives as well as the commander's vision.

Example from ADRP 5-0

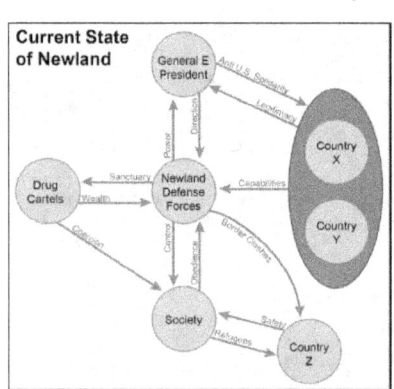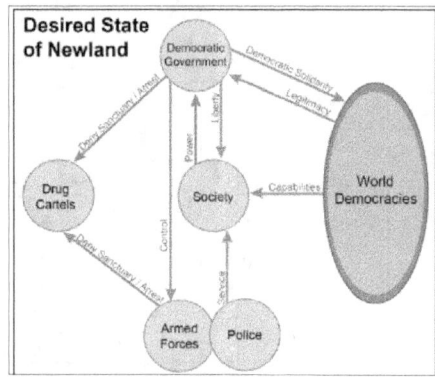

Developing the Problem Statement

- The problem should be framed in terms of time, space, purpose, and resources.
- The problem statement should remain broad. It shouldn't include tasks that box in the commander.

Example Problem Statement (ADRP 5-0)

The Newland defense force is the primary impediment to establishing a democratic government in Newland and the primary factor of instability in the region. For over forty years, the Newland defense force has maintained power for itself and the regime by oppressing all opposition within society. In addition, the Newland defense force has a history of intimidating Country Z through force (both overtly and covertly). Corruption in the Newland defense force is rampant within the leadership, and it has close ties to several drug cartels. General E is the latest of two dictators emerging from the Newland defense force. Even if General E is removed from power, the potential of a new dictator emerging from the Newland defense force is likely. There is no indication that the leadership of the Newland defense force is willing to relinquish their power within Newland.

Developing the Operational Approach

- The operational approach should be informed by the commander's guidance.
- Utilize the elements of operational art to help develop and frame the broad operational approach.

Example Operational Approach (ADRP 5-0)

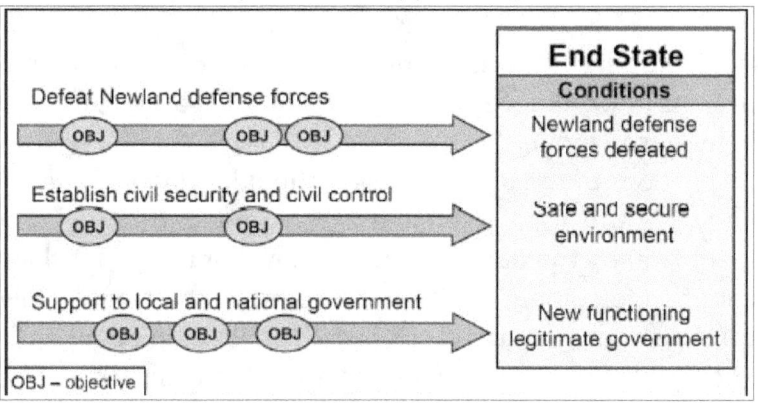

Common Reasons for Reframing (ADRP 5-0)

- The future assessment reveals a lack of progress
- Key assumptions prove invalid
- Unanticipated success or failure
- An event causes a "catastrophic change" in the operational environment
- A scheduled periodic review
- A change in mission or end state issued by higher authority

Recommended Operational Environment/Problem Framing Brief (Optional)

- Title slide
- Purpose of the brief
- Agenda
- Planning guidance
- Inputs – Orders/CO Guidance/INSUMs/Strategic context
- Operational Environment
  - o Internal cycle model
  - o External cycle model
  - o Temporal model
  - o Spatial model
- Comments/Questions

Notes
- While not in current doctrine, providing the commander options prior to developing the operational approach is helpful (see models).
- All portions of the design process should include both a narrative and visual to enable the commander's visualization.
- Identify early the desired structure level of design for the commander. Some prefer white board "discussions" while others prefer formalized briefings with Power Point.
- The problem statement should inform the evaluating criteria.

Recommended Operational Approach Brief (Optional)
- Title slide
- Purpose of the brief
- Agenda
- Planning guidance
- Inputs – Orders/CO Guidance/INSUMs/Strategic context
- Operational Environment (any updates)
- Operational Approach (graphic)
- Proposed Intent
- Comments/Questions

Joint Operational Design

Reference: JP 5-0

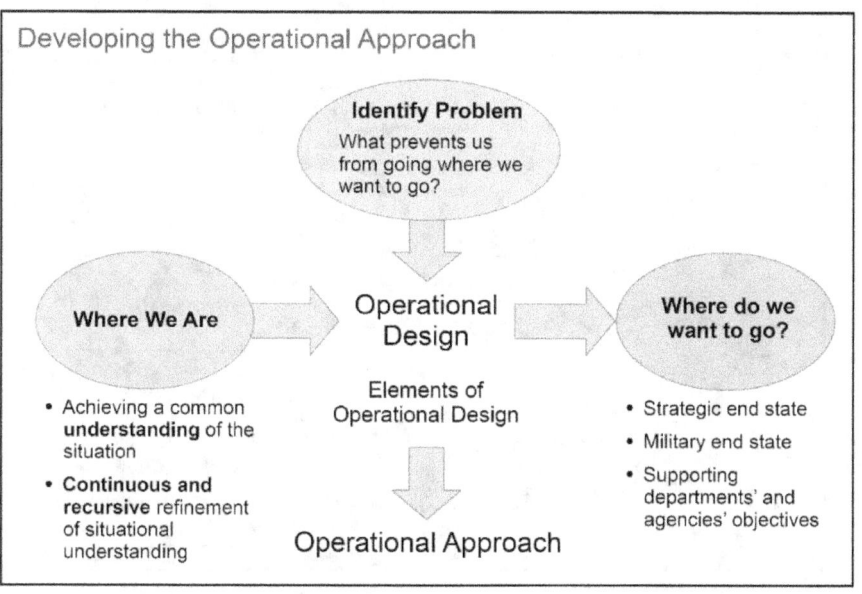

Campaign Design

Reference: TRADOC PAM 525-5-500

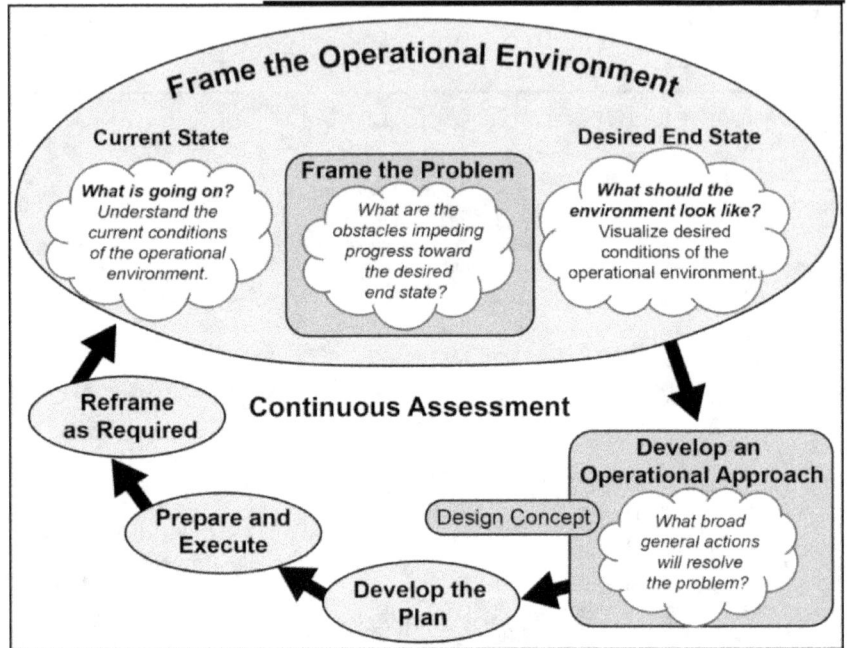

Problem Framing

- Establish the strategic context
- Synthesize strategic guidance
- Describe the systemic nature of the problem(s) to be solved
- Determine strategic trends
- Identify gaps in knowledge
- Establish assumptions about the problem
- Identify the operational problem
- Determine the initial mission statement
- Obtain approval of the problem and mission statement

NATO Design

Reference: Allied Command Operations Comprehensive
Operations Planning Directive COPD Interim V2.0 (OCT13)

NATO operational design is fundamental to:
- Communicate the Commander's initial intent for the
  campaign or operation
- Provide the common basis for COA development
- Develop the provisional missions for components
- Synchronize and coordinate the campaign over time in
  coordination with national and international actors
- Assess progress or delay of the campaign
- Adapt and adjust the OPLAN to deal with
  foreseen/unforeseen events

With slight variations in verbiage, the actual design process
mirrors the United States processes. NATO headquarters typically
use the process at the operational and strategic levels.

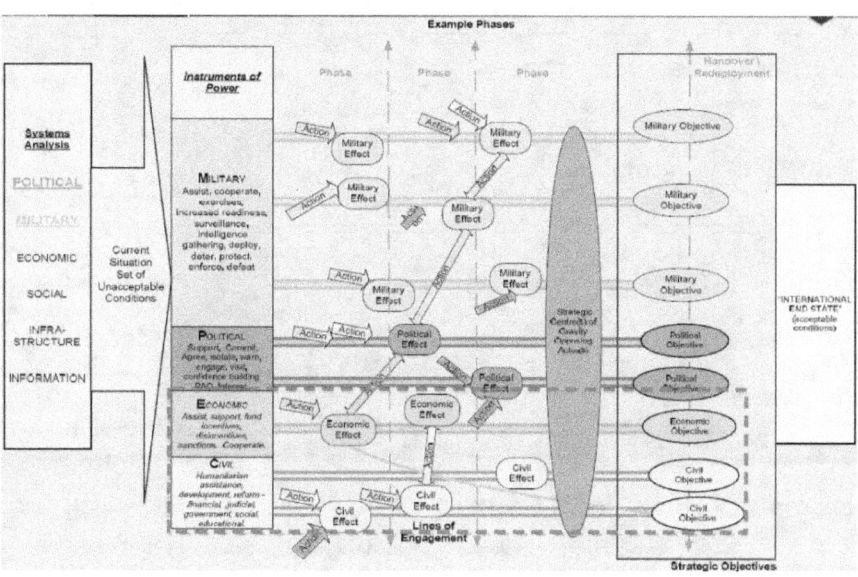

Strategic Design

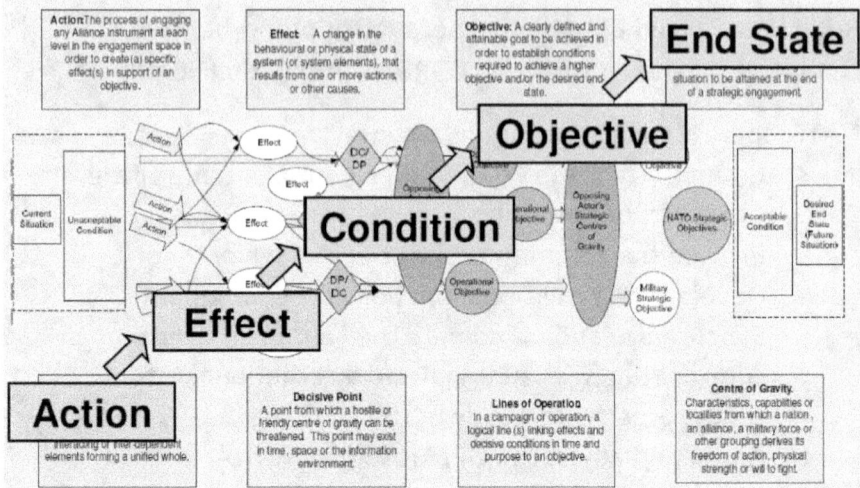

Transition to Operational Design

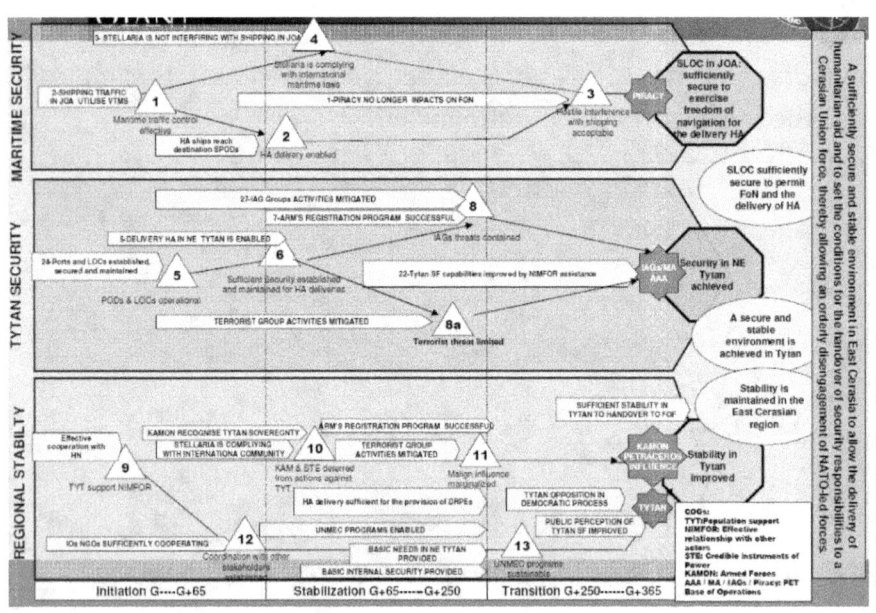

Example of Operational Design

Chapter 4 – Model Playbook

A model is a representative system or thing used to replicate a structure, process, or thing. Within the military context, most reporting formats, checklists, and diagrams within doctrine are systems developed from experience. Because they are merely a replication, a solitary model is statically ineffective for predicting future actions. For actionable, accurate prediction, utilize multiple models.

This section provides an assortment of doctrinal and non-doctrinal model to assist in quickly referencing potential models for problem solving and planning.

Doctrinal

Engagement Area Development

Description: These steps enable the leader to create an engagement area regardless of being in the offense or defense.
Origin: FM 3-21.8 (MAR07)

Step	Element
1	Identify all likely enemy avenues of approach.
2	Determine likely enemy schemes of maneuver.
3	Determine where to kill the enemy.
4	Plan and integrate obstacles.
5	Emplace weapon systems.
6	Plan and integrate indirect fires.
7	Rehearse the execution of operations in the EA.

Elements of Operational Art

The elements of operational art assist in framing the operational approach.

Origin: ADRP 5-0 (MAY12)

Elements	
End State/Conditions	Center of Gravity
Decisive Points	Lines of Operations
Lines of Effort	Operational Reach
Basing	Tempo
Phasing	Transitions
Culmination	Risk

Elements of Operational Design

The elements of operational design assist in framing the operational approach in joint design.

Origin: JP 5-0 (AUG11)

Elements	
Termination	Direct/Indirect Approach
Military End State	Anticipation
Objectives	Operational Reach
Effects	Culmination
Center of Gravity	Arranging Operations
Decisive Points	Forces and Functions
Lines of Operations	Lines of Effort

Lines of Operation

Description: Lines of operation display the sequence of actions within an operation.
Origin: JP 5-0 (AUG11)

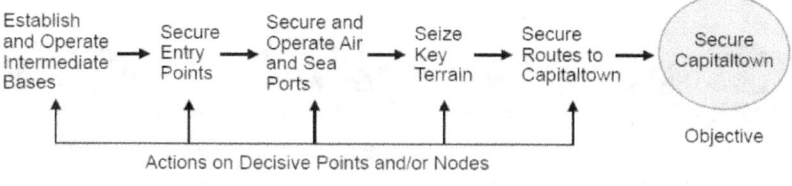

Sample Line of Operation

Warfighting Functions

Description: They are a group of tasks and systems to assist in accomplishing missions.
Origin: ADP 3-0 (OCT11)

Functions	
Mission Command	Fires
Movement and Maneuver	Sustainment
Intelligence	Protection

Defeat/Stability Mechanisms

Description: Defeat and stability mechanisms describe how friendly forces accomplish their assigned mission. They are not tactical missions but describe the broad operational and tactical effects.

Origin: ADRP 3-0 (MAY12)

Defeat Mechanisms	Stability Mechanisms
Destroy: applying lethal combat power on an enemy capability so that it can no longer perform any function (it must be completely rebuilt to become usable)	*Compel*: to use, or threaten the use of, lethal force to establish control and dominance, effect behavioral change, or enforce compliance with mandates, agreements, or civil authority
Dislocate: employing forces to obtain significant positional advantage, rendering the enemy's dispositions less valuable	*Control*: imposing civil order
Disintegrate: disrupting the enemy's command and control system, degrading its ability to conduct operations (leads to rapid collapse of the capabilities or will to fight)	*Influence*: altering the opinions, attitudes, and ultimately behavior of foreign friendly, neutral, adversary, and enemy populations through inform and influence activities, presence, and conduct
Isolate: denying an enemy or adversary access to capabilities that enable the exercise of coercion, influence, potential advantage, and freedom of action	*Support*: establish, reinforce, or set the conditions necessary for the instruments of national power to function effectively

Lines of Effort

Description: Lines of effort frame the operation in terms of consecutive efforts.

Origin: JP 5-0 (AUG11)

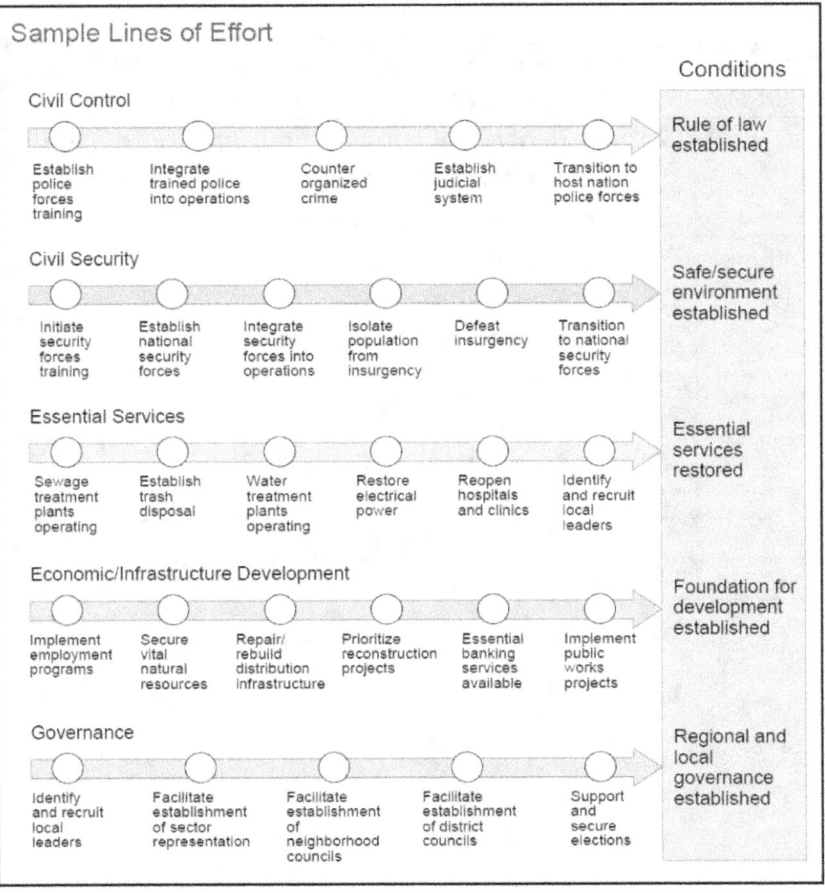

Classes of Supply

Description: The ten classes of supply are utilized to describe requirements.

Origin: BCTC Battle Staff Guide (AUG10)

Class	Description
I	Subsistence; includes health and welfare
II	Clothing, individual equipment, tents, tools, hand tools, administrative and housekeeping supplies; does not include major property book items
III	POL, petroleum and solid fuels
IV	Construction material
V	Ammunition, bombs, explosives, mines, fuses, and projectiles
VI	Personal demand items
VII	Major property book end items
VIII	Medical material
IX	Repair parts and components
X	Material to support non-military programs

Army Operational Framework

Description: These four constructs enable description within planning. Army leaders are not bound by any specific framework but the frameworks have proven helpful either by themselves or in concert.

Origin: ADRP 3-0 (MAY12)

Construct	Components
Deep- Close- Security (Support)	Deep area: a forward area used to shape the enemy prior to them being encountered or engaged in the close area
	Close area: an area in which the commander conducts decisive action
	Support area: an area to the rear of the close area in which support functions are provided
	Security operations: provide early and accurate warning of enemy operations
Decisive- Shaping- Sustaining	Decisive operation: an operation that directly accomplishes the mission
	Shaping operation: an operation that establishes conditions for the decisive operation through effects on the enemy, other actors, and the terrain
	Sustaining operation: an operation that enables the decisive operation or shaping operation by generating or maintaining combat power
Main and Supporting Efforts	Main effort: element that has the most critical mission to the overall operation at a specific time
	Supporting effort: an element with a mission that supports the success of the main effort

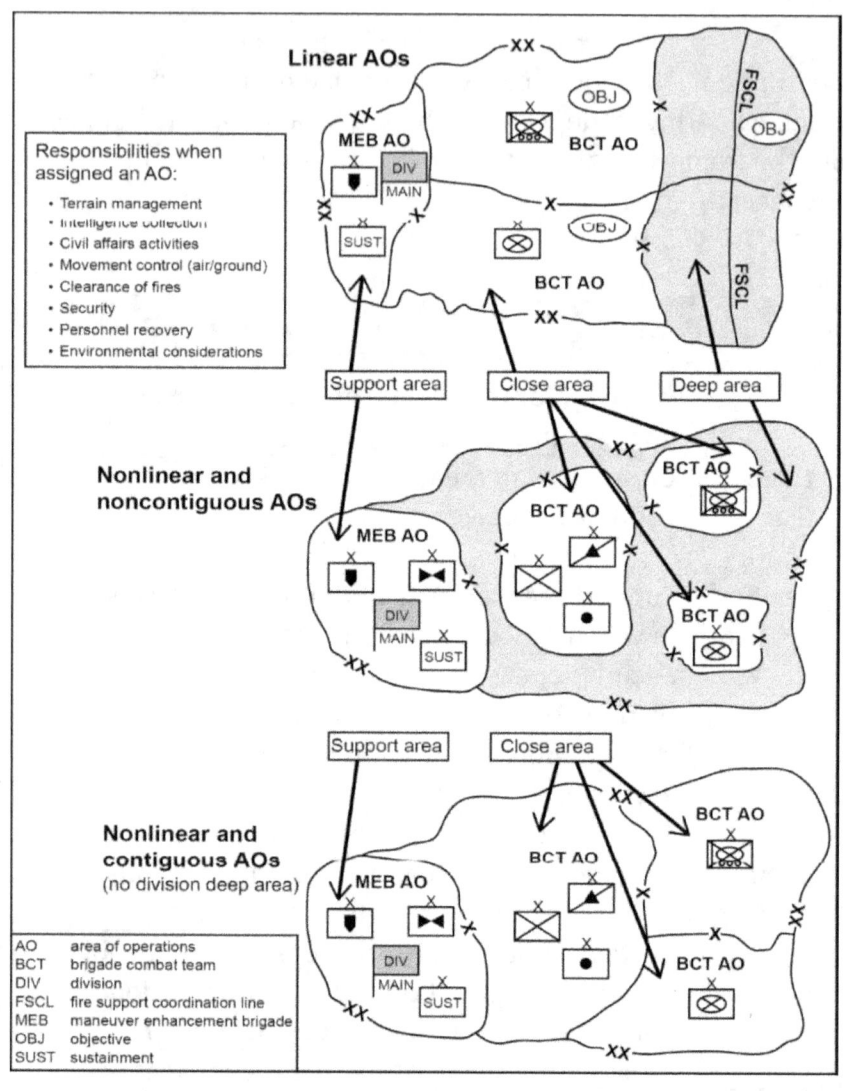

Linear AOs

Responsibilities when assigned an AO:

- Terrain management
- Intelligence collection
- Civil affairs activities
- Movement control (air/ground)
- Clearance of fires
- Security
- Personnel recovery
- Environmental considerations

MEB AO

DIV MAIN

SUST

BCT AO

OBJ

OBJ

FSCL

OBJ

BCT AO

Support area

Close area

Deep area

Nonlinear and noncontiguous AOs

MEB AO

DIV MAIN

SUST

BCT AO

BCT AO

BCT AO

BCT AO

Support area

Close area

Nonlinear and contiguous AOs
(no division deep area)

MEB AO

DIV MAIN

SUST

BCT AO

BCT AO

BCT AO

AO	area of operations
BCT	brigade combat team
DIV	division
FSCL	fire support coordination line
MEB	maneuver enhancement brigade
OBJ	objective
SUST	sustainment

4-76

PMESII/ASCOPE Crosswalk

Description: The PMESII/ASCOPE crosswalk aligns two doctrinal operational variable constructs to better understand an area.
Origin: ADRP 3-90 (AUG12)

	P Political	M Military	E Economic	S Social	I Infrastructure	I Information
A Areas						
S Structures						
C Capabilities						
O Organizations						
P People						
E Events						

Planning Variables

Description: SWEATMS and OAKOC provide frameworks for describing the physical environment.
Origin: FM 3-42.2 (APR09)

Sewer

Water

Electricity

Academic

Trash

Medical

Security

Observation & Fields of Fire
Avenues of Approach
Key Terrain
Obstacles
Cover & Concealment

Joint Phasing

Description: While JP 5-0 indicates that the phases are purely an example, they are often used as the doctrinal template for operations.
Origin: JP 5-0 (2011)

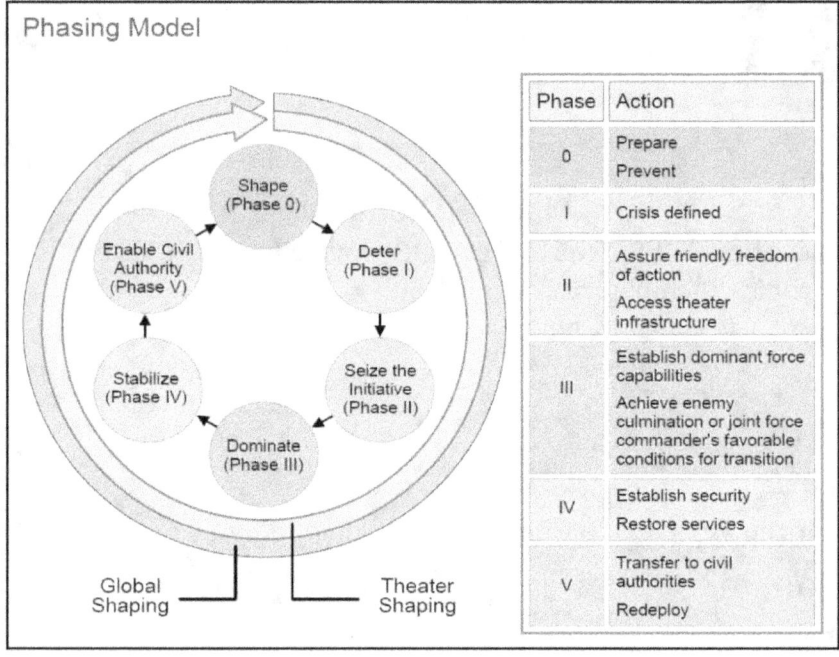

Center of Gravity

Description: Center of gravity is a concept that is highly debated in the military. As a tool, it identifies both vulnerabilities of friendly and enemy forces.
Origin: On War, JP 5-0 (2011)

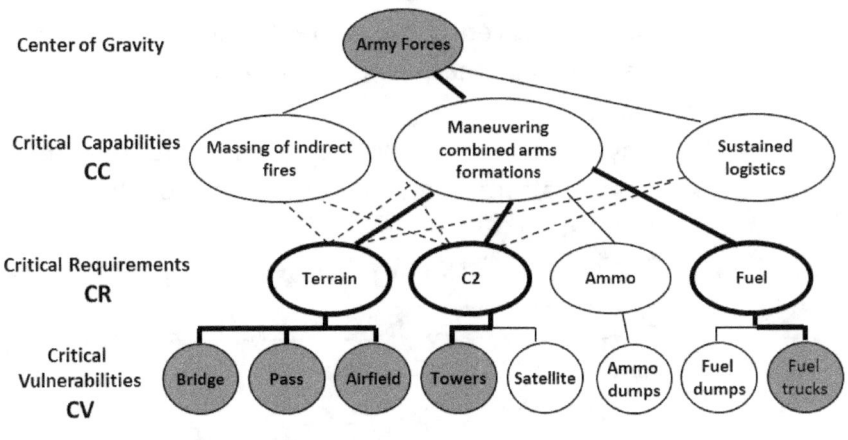

Modified Combined Obstacle Overlay

Description: The MCOO provides a visual representation of terrain effects on a map. The OAKOC framework is typically used to develop and brief the MCOO.

Origin: FM 2-01.3 (OCT09)

- Severely restricted terrain
    - Severely hinders or slows movement in combat formations
    - Usually marked with cross-hatched diagonal lines
- Restricted terrain
    - Hinders movement to some degree
    - Usually depicted with diagonal lines
- Key terrain
    - Any locality or area whose seizure, retention, or control affords a marked advantage to either combatant
    - Typically depicted by a purple circle 'K'

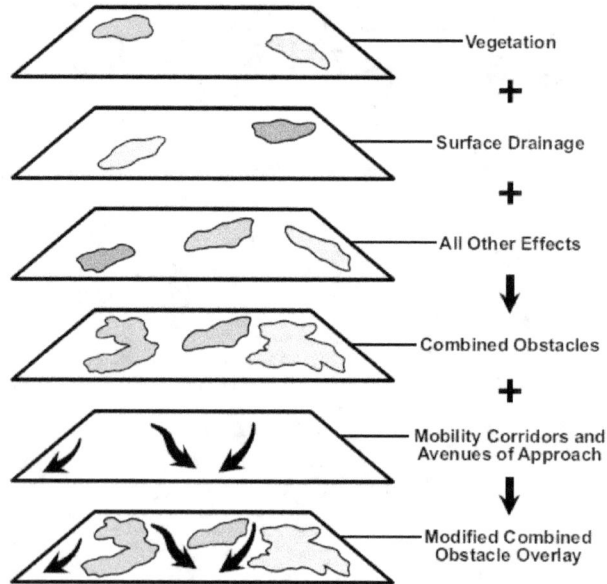

Decision Support Matrix (DSM)

Description: It is a written record of a war-gamed course of action that describes decision points and associated actions at those decision points.

Origin: ADRP 5-0 (MAY12)

COA 2 DECISION SUPPORT MATRIX						
PLAN			DECIDE	EXECUTE		ASSESS
CCIR Type / #	Reporting Agency	NAI #	DP #	Branch Plan # (task-purpose & associated TAI's)	Conditions Desired	Measures of Effectiveness (Indicators & pertinent information)
1 ⭐1	RECON, JSTARS, IMINT, JFACC	1,9,12,17	Do we take AoA on RTE 12 or AoA 2 on RTE 3 to OBJ LEE?		If WAC reserve not destroyed by JFACC and LR fires, disposition and location of 91st and 93rd MECH BDEs required to determine which route for ME.	ID WAC reserve on RTE 12 and/or RTE 3. What is disposition and strength or 6th ID or 12th ID on RTE 12?
1,8,12 ⭐2	RECON, JSTARS, IMINT	3,8,9,11,1 2,13	Do we commit the Amphibious Reserve?		Friendly forces committed to MSR SPORTING and unable to advance to OBJ LEE. WAC Reserve already committed.	Status of units along RTE 03 Status of eastern landing beach south of OBJ Pickett.
1 ⭐3	RECON, JSTARS, IMINT, JFACC	1,8,9,17	If the WAC Reserve remains in vic. MUAR, do we attack their position after OBJ LEE is secure?		OBJ LEE is secure and WAC Reserve remains in AAs vic MUAR.	WAC Reserve fixed vic MUAR.
⭐4	RECON, JSTARS, IMINT, JFACC	1.8.9.17	Do we cross south of PL Red to posture on PL White?		OBJ LEE is secure and WAC Reserve remains in AA vic MUAR.	WAC Reserve fixed vic. MUAR.

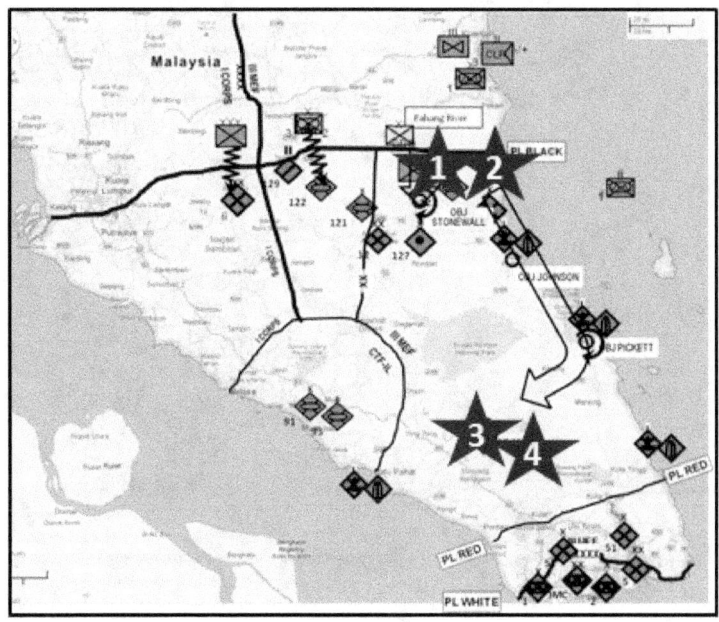

4-81

Threat/Adversary Template

Description: Threat/adversary templates, traditionally called doctrinal templates (DOCTEMPs), graphically portray how the threat/adversary might utilize its capabilities to perform the functions required to accomplish its objectives.

Origin: FM 2-01.3 (OCT09)

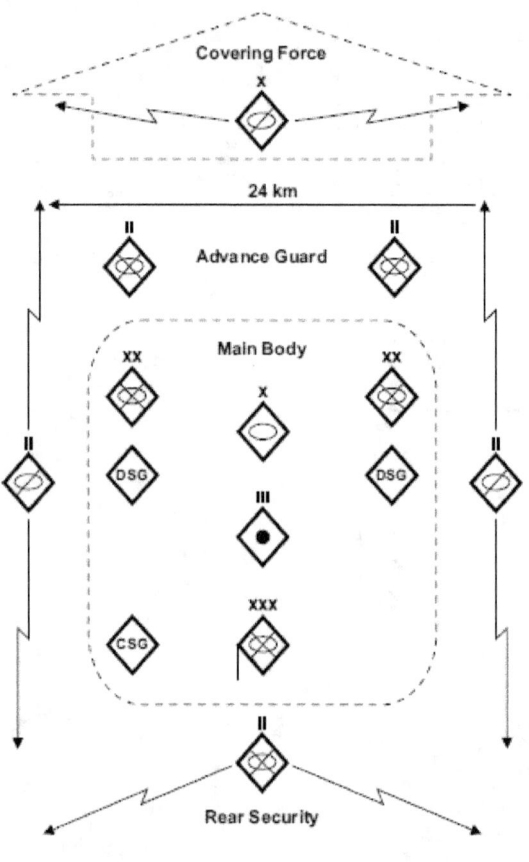

Situation Template (SITEMP)

Description: This model is built applying the adversary's current situation in terms of the threat/adversary template.

Origin: FM 2-01.3 (OCT09)

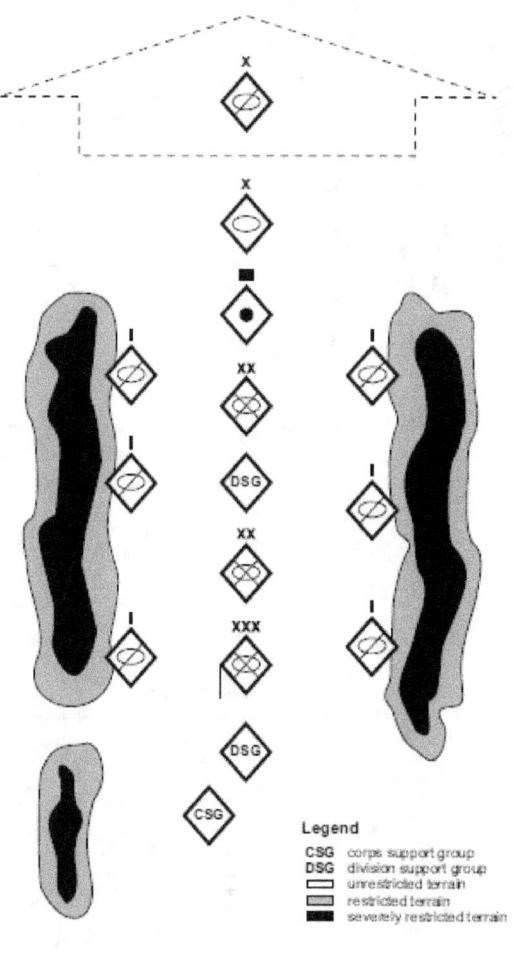

Legend

CSG corps support group
DSG division support group
☐ unrestricted terrain
▨ restricted terrain
■ severely restricted terrain

Event Template (EVENTTEMP)

Description: The event template guides ISR synchronization and ISR planning by using NAIs to indicate the threat COA.

Origin: FM 2-01.3 (OCT09)

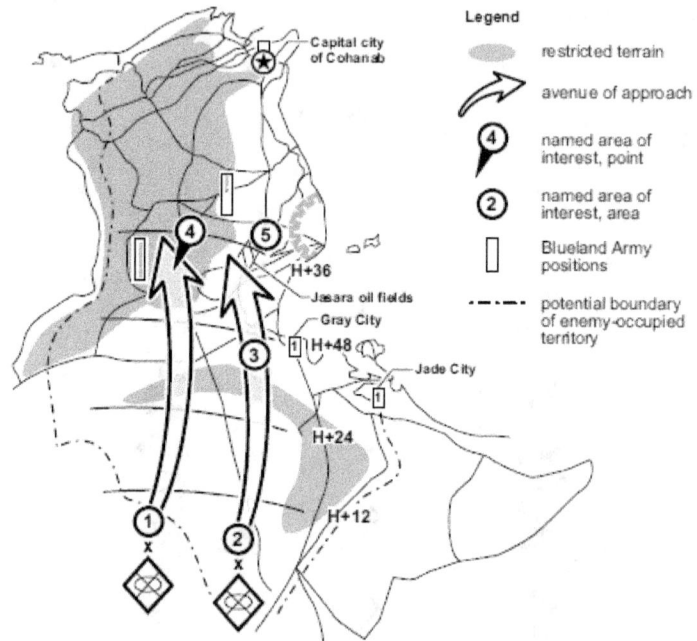

Figure E-4. Event Template.

Table E-3. Event Matrix.

Named Area of Interest	No Earlier Than	No Later Than	Event/Indicator
1	H+6	H+12	Brigade-sized forces moving north.
2	H+6	H+12	Brigade-sized forces moving north.
3	H+12	H+24	Orangeland forces enter Blueland. Northern operational group driving on Jesara oil fields.
4	H+14	H+24	Orangeland forces seize junction of highways 7 and 8. Northern operational group turns northwest toward Jesara.
5	H+18	H+24	Orangeland forces enter Tealton. Northern operational group driving on Jesara.

Mass Atrocity Response Operations Approaches

Description: One or more of the following approaches can be utilized in peacekeeping operations.

Origin: JP 3-07.3 (AUG12)

MASS ATROCITY RESPONSE OPERATIONS APPROACHES

Approach	Characteristics	Considerations
Approach 1 Area Security	• Wide area control • Unit sectors • Mobile patrols • Quick response forces (QRFs) • Outposts • Mobile Operating Base	• Requires adequate forces, extensive logistics, and weak adversary • Suitable when victim population is widely dispersed • Extensive stability operations necessary
Approach 2 Shape, Clear, Hold, Build	• Clear-hold-build • Focused, systematic advance within capabilities • "Mobile" forces clear; "static" forces maintain security	• Fewer forces required than Area Security Approach • Suitable with strong perpetrators and concentrated victim populations • Cedes territory to perpetrators • Extended commitment
Approach 3 Separation	• Controlled buffer zone between perpetrators and victims • Outposts, patrols, and QRFs • Supporting fires, as required • Similar to traditional peacekeeping or demilitarized zone operations	• Limited forces required • Suitable when perpetrators and victims are separated • Cedes territory to perpetrators • Forces may be caught between belligerent groups • Potential long-term division
Approach 4 Safe Areas	• Protect internally displaced person camps • Secure areas of victim concentration • Defensive posture • Security on migration routes • Expect increased numbers of civilians who seek protection	• Limited forces required • Suitable when victims are concentrated • Cedes territory to perpetrators • Large humanitarian assistance burden • May "reward" perpetrators
Approach 5 Partner Enabling	• Most ground forces from coalition partners or victim groups • US provides security force assistance, equipment, or key enablers (deployment, air, conventional forces, special operations forces [SOF])	• Partners bear most burdens • Minimizes US footprint • Helps build indigenous capability • Partners may be less capable than US forces • US relinquishes control of effort
Approach 6 Containment	• Reliance on air, maritime, cyberspace, and SOF • No-fly zones, blockades, and strikes • Integrated with diplomatic and informational efforts	• Capitalizes on US military strengths (air, sea, cyberspace) • Limited in-country presence • Does not provide direct protection to victims • Risk of collateral damage • Precursor to other approaches
Approach 7 Defeat Perpetrators	• Offensive focus against perpetrators • Defeat perpetrator leadership and military capability • Regime change or collapse, if necessary	• Large force required • May be required for long-term resolution • Extensive stabilization effort and reconstruction support required • Potential for high casualties and collateral damage

Spaghetti Model

Description: The model links actors (state, organization, or individual) by different drivers.

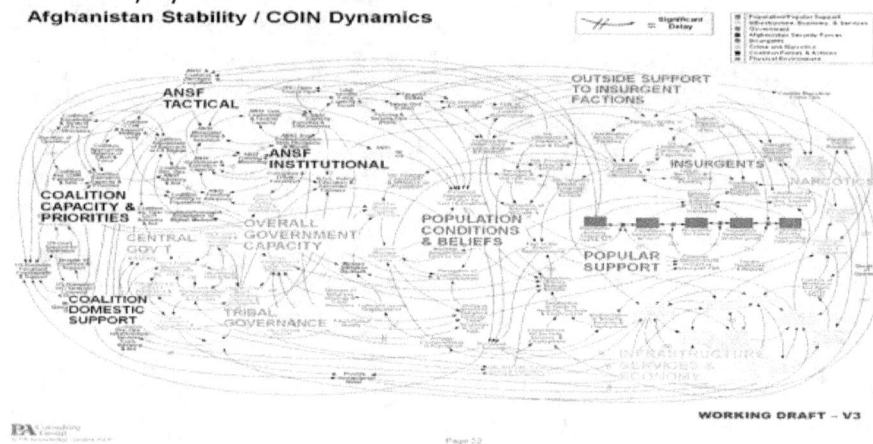

Timeline Analysis Model

Description: Overlay timelines to see the overlapping time analysis.

Origin: Dr. Stanley

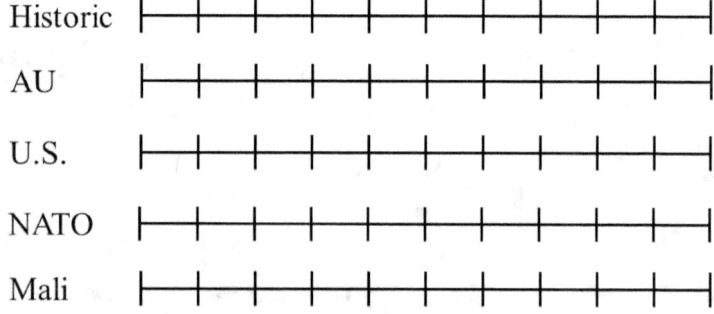

LOO Evolution Model

Description: This model is a simple method of transitioning LOOs from basic to conceptual.

Origin: Gary McDonald

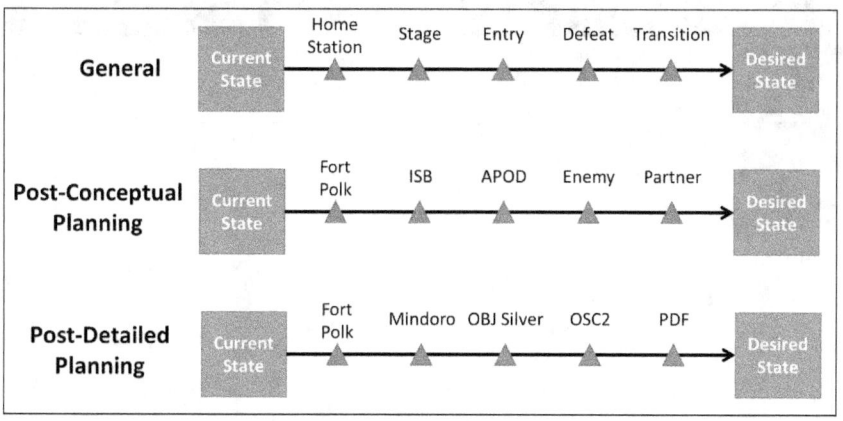

Option Generation Model

Description: Develops multiple options and their respective COAs. The option looks at different issues that must be solved.

Origin: Dr. Bruce Stanley

Option 1

	Purpose	Resources	Time	Space	Endstate	Risk
COA 1			When set/How long it would take			Mission/ Force
COA 2						
COA 3						
COA 4						

Burma Example

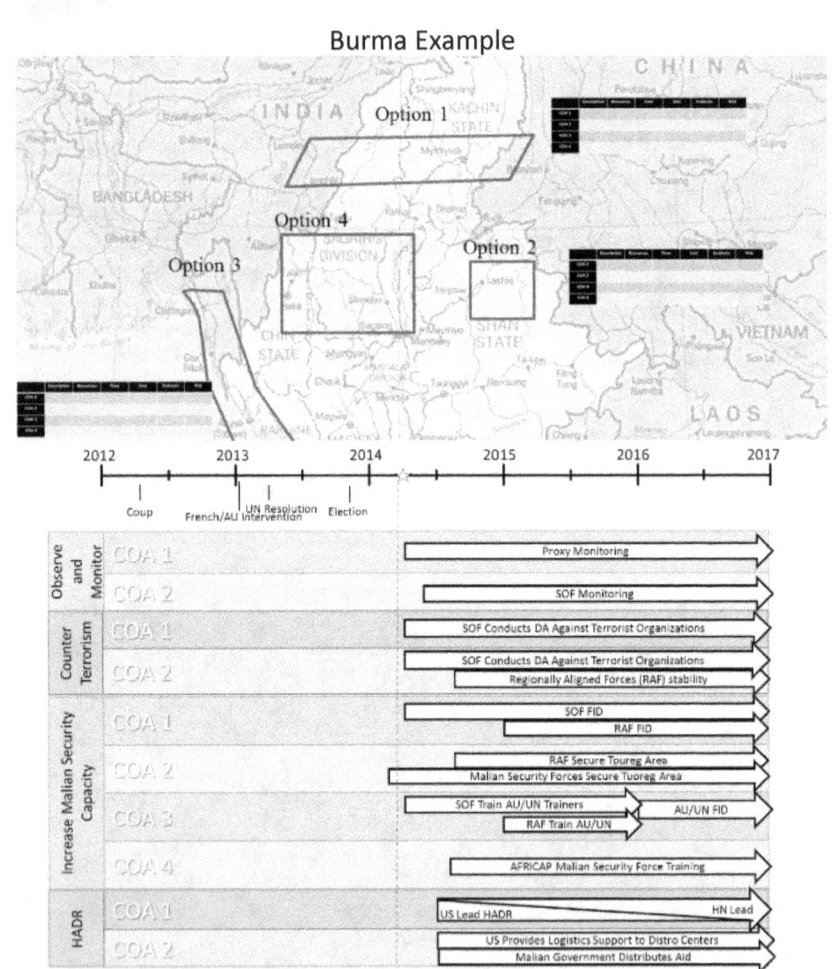

Description: Most commanders do not want their subordinates and staffs to give them a single course of action or even multiple courses of action with only a single option being feasible. They desire a concise well-developed menu of options to help in their decision making process. This was the letter developed by the joint staff for congress identifying possible options in Syria. Origin: General Martin Dempsey (19JUL13)

The Honorable Carl Levin
Chairman
Committee on Armed Services
United States Senate
Washington, DC 20510

Dear Mr. Chairman:

On 18 July 2013, you asked me to provide an unclassified assessment of options for the potential use of U.S. military force in the Syrian conflict. It offers my independent judgment with as much openness as this classification allows. I am mindful that deliberations are ongoing within our government over the further role of the United States in this complex sectarian war. The decision over whether to introduce military force is a political one that our Nation entrusts to its civilian leaders. I also understand that you deserve my best military advice on how military force could be use in order to decide whether it should be used.

At this time, the military's role is limited to helping deliver humanitarian assistance, providing security assistance to Syria's neighbors, and providing non-lethal assistance to the opposition. Patriot batteries are deployed to Turkey and Jordan for their defense against missile attack. An operational headquarters and additional capabilities, including F-16s, are positioned to defend Jordan. We are also prepared for the options described below:

Train, Advise, and Assist the Opposition. The option uses nonlethal forces to train and advise the opposition on tasks ranging from weapons employment to tactical planning. We could also offer assistance in the form of intelligence and logistics. The scale could range from several hundred to several thousand troops with the costs varying accordingly, but estimated at $500 million per year initially. The option requires safe areas outside Syria as well as support from our regional partners. Over time, the impacts would be the improvement in opposition capabilities. Risks include extremists gaining access to additional capabilities, retaliatory cross-border attacks, and insider attacks or inadvertent association with war crimes due to vetting difficulties.

Conduct Limited Standoff Strikes. This option uses lethal force to strike targets that enable the regime to conduct military operations, proliferate advanced weapons, and defend itself. Potential targets include high-value regime air defense, air, ground, missile, and naval forces as well as the supporting military facilities and command nodes. Standoff air and missile systems could be used to strike hundreds of aircraft, ships, submarines, and other enablers. Depending on duration, the costs would be in the billions. Over time, the impact would be the significant degradation of regime capabilities and an increase in regime desertions. There is a risk that the regime could withstand limited strikes by dispersing its assets. Retaliatory attacks are also possible, and there is a probability for collateral damage impacting civilians and foreigners inside the country.

Establish a No-Fly Zone. This option uses lethal force to prevent the regime from using its military aircraft to bomb and resupply. It would extend air superiority over Syria by neutralizing the regime's advanced, defense integrated air defense system. It would also shoot down adversary aircraft and strike airfields, aircraft on the ground, and supporting infrastructure. We would require hundreds of ground and sea-based aircraft, intelligence and electronic warfare support, and enablers for refueling and communications. Estimated costs are $500 million initially, averaging as much as a billion dollars per month over the course of a year. Impacts would likely include the near total elimination of the regime's ability to bomb opposition strongholds and sustain its forces by air. Risks include the loss of U.S. aircraft, which would require us to insert personnel recovery forces. It may also fail to reduce the violence or shift the momentum because the regime relies overwhelmingly on surface fires – mortars, artillery, and missiles.

Establish Buffer Zones. The option uses lethal and nonlethal force to protect specific geographic areas, most likely across the borders with Turkey and Jordan. The opposition could use these zones to organize and train. They could also serve as safe areas for the distribution of humanitarian assistance. Lethal force would be required to defend the zones against air, missile, and ground attacks. This would necessitate the establishment of a limited no-fly zone, with its associated resource requirements. Thousands of U.S. ground forces would be needed, even if positioned outside Syria, to support those physically defending the zones. A limited no-fly zone coupled with U.S. ground forces would push the costs over one billion dollars per month. Over time, the impact would be an improvement in opposition capabilities. Human suffering could also be reduced, and some pressure could be lifted off Jordan and Turkey. Risks are similar to the no-fly zone with the added problem of regime surface fires into the zones, killing more refugees due to their concentration. The zones could also become operational bases for extremists.

Control Chemical Weapons. This option uses lethal force to prevent the use or proliferation of chemical weapons. We do this by destroying portions of Syria's massive stockpile, interdicting its movement and delivery, or by seizing and securing program components. At a minimum, this option would call for a no-fly zone as well as air and missile strikes involving hundreds of aircraft, ships, submarines, and other enablers. Thousands of special operations forces and other ground forces would be needed to assault and secure critical sites. Costs could also average well over one billion dollars per month. The impact would be the control of some, but not all chemical weapons. It would also help prevent their further proliferation into the hands of extremist groups. Our ability to fully control Syria's storage and delivery systems could allow extremists to gain better access. Risks are similar to the no-fly zone with the added risk of U.S. boots on the ground.

Too often, these options are considered in isolation. It would be better if they were assessed and discussed in the context of an overall whole-of-government strategy for achieving our policy objectives in coordination with our allies and partners. To this end, I have supported a regional approach that would isolate the conflict to prevent regional destabilization and weapons proliferation. At the same time, we would help develop a moderate opposition – including their military capabilities – while maintaining pressure on the Assad regime.

All of these options would likely further the narrow military objective of helping the opposition and placing more pressure on the regime. We have learned from the past 10 years; however, that it is not enough to simply alter the balance of military power without careful consideration of what is necessary in order to preserve a functioning state. We must anticipate and be prepared for the unintended consequences of our actions. Should the regime's institutions collapse in the absence of a viable opposition, we could inadvertently empower extremists or unleash the very chemical weapons we seek to control.

I know that the decision to use force is not one any one of us takes lightly. It is no less than an act of war. As we weigh our options, we should be able to conclude with some confidence that the use of force will move us toward the intended outcome. We must also understand the risk – not just to our forces, but to our other global responsibilities. This is especially critical as we lose readiness due to budget cuts and fiscal uncertainty. Some options may not be feasible in time or cost without compromising our security elsewhere. Once we take action, we should be prepared for what comes next. Deeper involvement is hard to avoid. We should also act in accordance with the law, and to the extent possible, in concert with our allies and partners to share the burden and solidify the outcome.

Thank you for this opportunity to share my assessment. The classified versions of all the options described have been presented to the National Security Staff for consideration by the Principals and the President. They have also been presented to the Congress in several briefs including one recently provided by the Vice Chairman of the Joint Chiefs of Staff.

Sincerely,

MARTIN E. DEMPSEY
General, U.S. Army

Warden's 5 Rings

Description: The model was created to prioritize for targeting. This model was used to prioritize sorties during Desert Storm.

Origin: Col. John A. Warden III

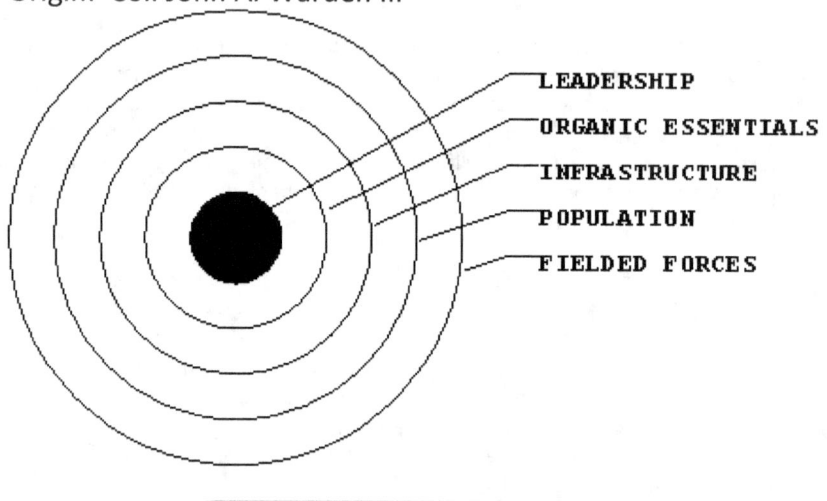

Trend Analysis

Description: This basic model plots incidents or data points to identify trends and outliers.

Origin: Various creators

Prisoner's Dilemma

Description: This model displays and analyzes the difference between rational (given current information) and best choice for individuals or organizations to identify the dominant strategy.

Origin: Merrill Flood and Melvin Dresher

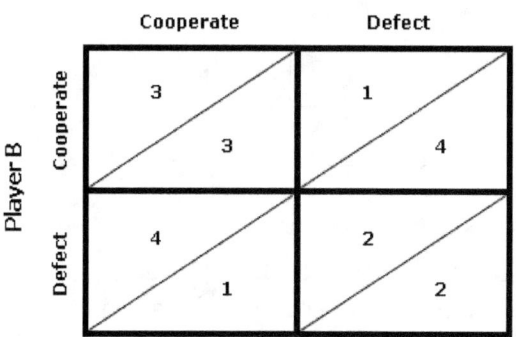

	Prisoner B stays silent (cooperates)	Prisoner B betrays (defects)
Prisoner A stays silent (cooperates)	Each serves 1 year	Prisoner A: 3 years Prisoner B: goes free
Prisoner A betrays (defects)	Prisoner A: goes free Prisoner B: 3 years	Each serves 2 years

Pure Coordination Game

Description: Games with multiple equilibria where players have identical preferences over the set of possible outcomes and where prominent/ conspicuous/ salient aspects of the equilibrium are removed to the extent possible.

	Left	Right
Left	10, 10	0, 0
Right	0, 0	10, 10

Fig. 2: Choosing sides

	Party	Home
Party	10, 10	0, 0
Home	0, 0	5, 5

Fig. 3: Pure coordination game

	Party	Home
Party	10, 5	0, 0
Home	0, 0	5, 10

Fig. 4: Battle of the sexes

	Stag	Hare
Stag	10, 10	0, 7
Hare	7, 0	7, 7

Fig. 5: Stag hunt

Issue/Risk Analysis

Description: Enables the user to visualize the issues on both levels in connection to both time and space to better understand the situation.

Origin: Dr. Stanley

	Strategic	Operational
Time		
Issues		
Space		
Issues		
Purpose		
Issues		

Chapter 5 - System Theory

The military uses System Theory as a baseline to develop understandings of interactions within both conceptual and detailed planning. By definition, System Theory is the accumulation of multiple theories across the spectrum of scientific specialties that ultimately define the traits and actions of systems. Ludwig von Bertanlanffy coined the term "system theory" in his book *General System Theory: Foundations, Development, Applications* in 1968. He further clarified that a system is a "set of elements standing in interrelation." The essence of system theory is the distinction between closed and open systems, and linear and non-linear systems. According to Bertalanffy, closed systems are systems that have been isolated from external factors while open remain affected by their surroundings. Linearity is described in terms of inputs and outputs. In a linear system, a predictable outcome is achieved when specific inputs are administered. A tangible example is an automobile. If the driver turns a key and the fluids are properly filled, there is a reasonable expectation that the engine will start. In contradiction, non-linear systems have cascading effects. The economy has a plethora of inputs, and undetermined outputs from a single interaction. A single input can cause an action that cascades through the system producing unexpected results or "outputs."

Linear Systems	Non-Linear Systems
Structurally Complex	Interactively Complex
Cause and Effect	Cascading Effect
Additive (Car)	Emergent Behavior (Ecosystem)
Constrained (fixed)	Freedom of Action (loose)
Computable	Not Computable
Closed	Open
Tends Toward Entropy	Negative Entropy

Independent	Interdependent
Study Systematically/Analytically	Study Systemically/Holistically
Static	Self-Organizing

General Concepts:

- The universe is the only true system, the rest are just mental models.
- Correlation is not Causality; if two separate occurrences are linked, the one does not necessarily rely on the other.
- The bounds and assumptions put on a non-linear system are crucial.
- A system can assume two or more states but a change in a parameter may cause a shift to another state.
- Understanding a system does not mean we can predict outcomes.
- Changing metaphors changes the way you look at things.
- Heisenberg principle – you may change the system by observing it.
- You can't understand a system from within the system.
- An action will never have only a single effect.
- Titanic Effect – after counteracting a risk, more risk is taken.
- Indirect effects may be more important than direct ones.
- Systems effects change as actors learn about them and about other's beliefs about them.
- Lijphart Effect – due to possible instability, the actor takes steps in anticipation which create artificial stability
- Domino Theory Paradox – Even small defeats produce positive feedback because the state's adversaries or allies will infer that it is weak and prone to retreat in other conflicts.

Key Terms/Definitions:

- Additive – individual parts can be manipulated independently
- Bifurcation – a division into two different parts
- Butterfly Effect – a butterfly in Singapore could cause a thunderstorm in New York
- Co-evolution – when something evolves and forces something else to evolve
- Emergent Properties – the whole is different from, not greater than, the sum of its parts
- Fractals – A way of seeing to infinity; self-similar; came to stand for a way of describing, calculating, and thinking about shapes that are irregular and fragmented
- Heuristics – rules of thumb
- Holism – the sum of the parts will not necessarily produce the desired effects
- Intractable Problems – Problems that are not solvable.
- Mental Models – people can't hold the world in their minds, just mental models
- Non-computable – these problems yield answers which are infinite (an example is the square root of 2)
- Open System/Closed System – Allowing/not allowing outside influence
- Period doubling – uses bifurcation
- Phase Space – a specific timeframe; where strange attractors live
- Phase Transitions – a macroscopic behavior that's hard to predict by looking at microscopic details; water to gas
- Predication – attribution of specific qualities; links certain qualities to particular subjects through the use of predicates and the adverbs and adjectives that modify them; "irregular war"
- Presupposition – background knowledge that is taken to be true; in doing so the individual creates a certain type of world

- Punctuated Equilibrium – one thing pushes something into a new space; the action will occur but at an undeterminable time; rice through a funnel
- Reductionism – reducing complexity to create simplicity; often reductionism overlooks crucial factors in systems
- Self-Organizing – tendency toward order; requires feedback; stadium clapping;
- Self-Similar – standing between two mirrors; symmetry across scale; pattern inside of a pattern
- Strange Attractors – those things that are always linked; systems tend toward them
- Subject Positioning – the relationship between subjects and objects
- System – a set of units or elements where a change of an element or a relationship produces other changes in the system; the entire system exhibits properties and behaviors that are different from those of the parts
- Systematic – study quantitatively using the scientific method
- Systemic – study qualitatively through various heuristic (self-learning) approaches

Bibliography

Headquarters, Department of Defense. *Joint Operation Planning*. JP 5-0.
Washington, DC: Headquarters Department of Defense, August 2011.

Headquarters, Department of Defense. *Peace Operations*. JP 3-07.3.
Washington, DC: Headquarters Department of Defense, August 2012.

Headquarters U.S. Army. *BCTC Battle Staff Guide*. Washington, DC:
Headquarters U.S. Army, August 2010.

Headquarters U.S. Army. *CALL Staff Officer's Quick Reference Guide*.
Washington, DC: Headquarters U.S. Army, January 2013.

Headquarters U.S. Army. *Commander and Staff Officer Guide*. ATTP 5-0.1.
Washington, DC: Headquarters U.S. Army, September 2011.

Headquarters U.S. Army. *Commander's Appreciation and Campaign Design*.
TRADOC PAM 525-5-500. Washington, DC: Headquarters U.S. Army,
January 2008.

Headquarters U.S. Army. *The Infantry Rifle Platoon and Squad*. FM 3-21.8.
Washington, DC: Headquarters U.S. Army, March 2007.

Headquarters U.S. Army. *Intelligence Officer's Handbook*. TC 2-50-5.
Washington, DC: Headquarters U.S. Army, January 2010.

Headquarters U.S. Army. *Intelligence Preparation of the Battlefield*. FM 2-01.3.
Washington, DC: Headquarters U.S. Army, October 2009.

Headquarters U.S. Army. *Offense and Defense*. ADRP 3-90. Washington, DC:
Headquarters U.S. Army, August 2012.

Headquarters U.S. Army. *Offense and Defense*. FM 3-90. Washington, DC:
Headquarters U.S. Army, July 2001.

Headquarters U.S. Army. *The Operations Process*. ADRP 5-0. Washington, DC:
Headquarters U.S. Army, May 2012.

Headquarters U.S. Army. *The Operations Process*. FM 5-0. Washington, DC: Headquarters U.S. Army, January 2005.

Headquarters U.S. Army. *Reconnaissance and Cavalry Squadron*. FM 3-90.96. Washington, DC: Headquarters U.S. Army, March 2010.

Headquarters U.S. Army. *Reconnaissance, Security, and Tactical Enabling Tasks*. FM 3-90.2. Washington, DC: Headquarters U.S. Army, March 2013.

Headquarters U.S. Army. *Tactics in Counterinsurgency*. FM 3-42.2. Washington, DC: Headquarters U.S. Army, April 2009.

Headquarters U.S. Army. *Unified Land Operations*. ADRP 3-0. Washington, DC: Headquarters U.S. Army, May 2012.

MAGTF Staff Training Program. *Operational Planning Team Leader's Guide*. Quantico, VA: MSTP, May 2012.

www.ingramcontent.com/pod-product-compliance
Lightning Source LLC
Chambersburg PA
CBHW071213280526
45787CB00002B/667

agarics, fungi like the mushroom, differing from each other in matters of form and color chiefly, the attachment of stipe and gills, the stability and instability of the entire structure. Some, as the "ink-caps" (*Coprinus*), spring in the night and vanish in inky dissolution ere the sun ascends to midday; others, as the little woolly fungus with cleft gills (*Schizophyllum*), so common on fallen branches everywhere, survive the storms of many seasons and outlast the substratum on which they grow. Fig. 3 shows the elegant curvature of the cleft gill-plates, and the order in which they appear. New ones are constantly intercalated between those already formed.

FIG. 3.—SCHIZOPHYLLUM COMMUNE.

In all these the lamellæ run out in rays and remain quite generally distinct from one another; but here follows a series in which these plates all intersect, or wander in many a winding line and labyrinthine pattern (*Dædalea, Trametes,* etc.), until the intersections become so numerous as to form a perfect honey-comb whose cells are minute pores. The gummy, golden *Boleti* of the woodlands, and the common bracket-fungi (*Polyporus*) of every stump and log in all the forest, are examples.

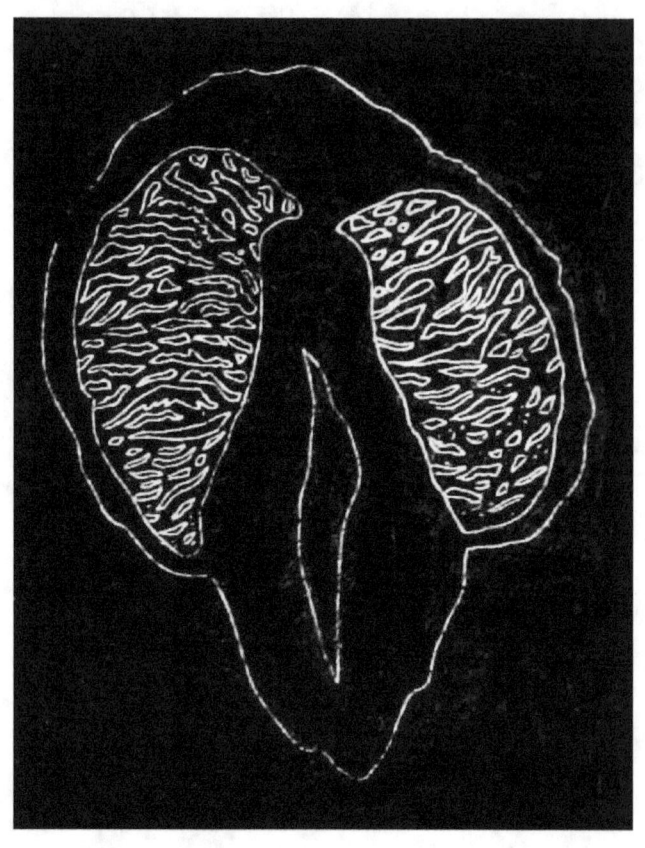

FIG. 4.—SECOLIUM WARNEI, vertical section.

Even the puff-ball family—another section of the greater fungi—form their fruit in agaric fashion, and the connection between our mushroom and the giant "louffer," though at first sight remote, is yet not far to seek. It must be remembered that mushrooms when first emerging from the ground are quite contracted and closed, often like a closed umbrella—one of the old-fashioned sort, puckered around the margin with a string. Split such a mushroom at this stage, and all the lamellæ will be found with their edges close pressed against the sides of the stipes, the edge of the pileus close drawn round the bottom. Now, in autumn we may find a fungus looking exactly like an unopened toad-stool; but you watch its opening in vain—it never opens.

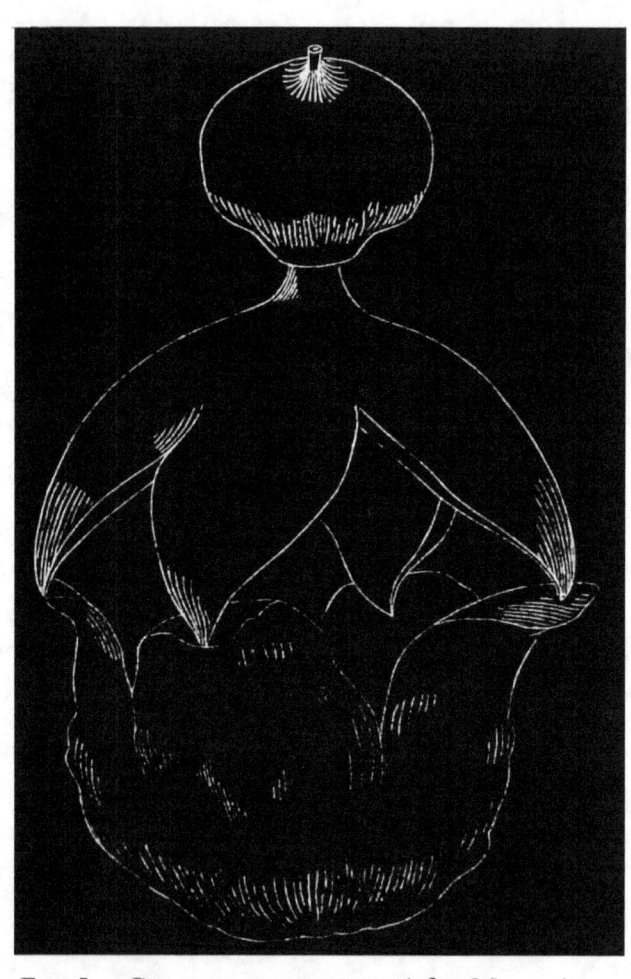

FIG. 5.—GEASTER FORNICATUS (after Morgan).

The puckering string never relaxes, the lamellae never leave the stipe, but are indeed grown fast against it, and with maturity become wrinkled in myriad folds, finally to break down entirely, leaving a mass of dusty brown spores which escape only with the final rupture of the fragile, unexpanded pileus (Fig. 4). From such a fungus the puff-ball differs chiefly in degree; the spores are borne upon threads and fill up definite cavities, one or more, and are discharged, as in the case just described, by the rupture of the inclosing tissues.

These latter here constitute a definite wall—the *peridium*. This may break open irregularly, or it may break regularly, throwing back from the top its pointed lobes in roseate and star-like forms—earth-stars, beautiful as they are curious, and offering a singularly perfect mechanism for the dispersal of the spores. Here is an earth-star (Fig. 5) whose peridium consists of three coats—two outer, strong and leathery, and one inner, delicate, silk-like.

The whole structure is developed as a smooth white ball beneath the soil. But, once the spores are ripe, the outermost peridium splits open at the top, its lobes spring backward and outward, giving room for the second covering to burst in similar fashion. The lobes of the second, however, by recurving, hoist the entire inner structure out of the ground and up into the air, where the inner peridium, enthroned thus upon springing arches, groined by no human hand, opens at tip a purse-like mouth, and suffers the spores slowly to escape, to sail on unknown journeys with the passing breeze.

We have space left but sufficient to mention the fruiting of the morel. Here we have on the outer upper side of the structure a layer of rather large elongate cells, quite similar to those on the mushroom gills; but, instead of abstricted spores on the outside of the supporting cells, we find each of the latter a fruit-case in which are lodged eight elliptical sporules arranged in a row, formed freely — that is, each entirely independent of the other and of the cell-wall that incloses all. But this method of fruiting brings us in sight of the microscopic and parasitic world of fungi, subject of our next chapter. Here, then, we well might rest; and yet, ere toadstools, mushrooms, and puffers vanish entirely from our thought, it were well to note, if but for a moment, the various titles these organisms wear. The names by which natural objects are known contain often in primary significance something of historic epitome; so, in the present case, we may discover the manner in which the object named first attracted human attention: the word itself is the record. Thus it appears that the word *fungus,* although coming to us from the Latin, is nevertheless of Greek origin, and is the same word as that we have anglicized in *sponge;* so that, according to the earliest record we have, the sponges of the sea and the fungi (puff-balls?) of the land were considered kin.

Our Teutonic ancestors seem to have arrived at the same conclusion; and to this day, for a German, *Schwamm* is either a sponge or a fungus, as you like it. Nor less interesting is the etymology of our other common names for such plants. Toadstool is sufficiently plain, prosaic, and suggestive; mushroom would seem to be the English adaptation of a French word, *mousseron* (something growing in or among moss), evidently pronounced by Englishmen long before spelled, and evincing the fact that the quick French wit was first to discover the edible qualities of this as of so many other delicacies.

II.

MICROSCOPIC FORMS

The microscopic world is ever fair. In every department of research we revert to our instruments, certainly expecting to be charmed by beauty, whether of movement or mechanism. Rarely are we disappointed, certainly not in the realm of organic form. Here everything is beautiful, and, as the heavens to the astronomer, everything is clean. Even the rudest fungi offer no exception. In them the microscope finds no exception to the law of beauty.

The simplicity of structure noted in the previous article runs through nearly all, only varied a thousand times; but whether mycelial thread or spores, one or other or both conjoined, the result, as we hope by illustration here to show, is always symmetry and elegance itself.

To begin, let us revert to the lilac-bush, whose whitened leaves may readily afford illustration of mycelial webs and threads. By September, if not sooner, the entire foliage will have taken on its peculiar whiteness as if thickly dusted with chalk or flour. On certain leaves, however, appear suspicious-looking dark-brown specks or grains, very small, but plainly visible to the naked eye.

Removing some of these granules to the microscope, we find the field filled with tiny sculptured spheres ornamented with a profusion of long, interlocking filaments, starting out like so many extended radii of each sphere. A gentle pressure on the cover-glass breaks the sphere, and forthwith (Fig. 1) a dozen tiny sacs appear, each packed with, transparent oval nucleated spores, just such spores and quite such sacs as appeared in the fruiting surface of the morel, and we are ready with the botanist to call the granules fruit. Who could have guessed the contents of that sphere? But look again at those radiating ornamental filaments. Trace to its distal end a single ray, and see the grapnels by which the fertile globule we have studied holds fast to the surface of its host through storm and flood.

Notice the elegant curves, the symmetrical branching, fit model for the artist in arabesque or filigree! What more beautiful or more efficiently suggestive! (Fig. 2 *a.*)

Such is the lilac blight; but now that we have discoverd one such fungus, we may carry our inquiries to almost any extent. The neighboring cherry-tree will afford similar material for study and admiration. Here the appendages are simpler, and the fruit itself contains but a single sac with spores (Fig. 3 *a*).

The poplars and the willows show spherules whose appendages are simple hooks, so that the fruit is a minute bur of the teazel sort, fit for fairy carding (Fig. 2 *b*). The oak-leaf and the hazel bear appendages simpler still, the appendages being straight and needle shaped, ray-like, actinic; *Phyllactinia Léveillé* named it—lea-fray— the needles starting like rays of light from some effulgent center (Fig. 3 h).

During the early days of autumn we can hardly go amiss for the appendaged fungi such as just described. In the woodland, the pastures, by the road-side, in shade and in sun, a thousand white-flecked leaves attract the appreciative and only the appreciative eye. Minuteness removes from ordinary ken—and the world goes on! Besides, these parasites are not especially harmful, at least in the phases described, to their presumably unwilling hosts.

The pea-vine and the rose-bush may sometimes suffer, but generally the leaves attacked have pretty well done the season's work before the parasite attains its maximum, so that man's interest in the matter is not specially affected. There is, however, another and different set of leaf-fungi whose parasitism is decidedly more intimate, and consequently destructive of the host-plant, suicidal as such a policy would seem to be.

These latter, as indeed all the fungi already cited, are known as blights, and as such some species are already famous. The potato murrain, which has its place in civil history, is a very pretty little transparent branching fungus, so delicate that a breath destroys it. First becoming notorious in 1845, and during the famines of 1846 and 1847, it has been found and studied in all parts of the world for the forty years succeeding.

The lilac fungus is content to spread its mycelium over the surface of the lilac-leaves, absorbing its nourishment from the surface cells; but the potato mold; the *Phytophthora infestans* of the books, seems to reach every cell and every tissue, so that a whole potato-field once infested will go down as if smitten by the frost of night. Kindred fungi are upon many of the plants about us. *Peronospora viticola* attacks the leaves of the grape. In wet seasons it is not uncommon to see the wild grape-vines along our western streams completely white with this overwhelming assailant, nor are our Concord vineyards ever quite exempt. The mycelial filaments thread the soft interior tissues while fruiting hyphæ come forth in delicate tufts or pencils through the open stomata on the under surface of the leaf. It is pleasant to think that weeds of various kinds suffer from similar fungal invasions. Thus goosefoot (*Chenopodium, sp.*) bears every spring upon its earlier leaves a tiny parasite, which seen under our lenses seems a miniature forest, while the fruit masses itself in violet tinted patches plainly to be seen by the naked eye.

Even the evergreens, the cone-bearers, that ancient race of hardy conservatives, are compelled to pay tithes and tribute to these all-assailing Vandals. I suppose the cedars of Lebanon are not exempt! At all events, who has not seen our native cedars bending after some warm shower in June with orange-colored fruit, beautiful, but to the cedar costly as it is fair? (Fig. 4 a.) Cedar-apples, men say, and they are not a few who would insist that the cedar is actually blooming and fruiting. Such fruit has actually been planted—vain expectation. Cedar-apples are but the excrescences caused by the persistent development of a fungus parasitic upon branch or leaf; they are receptacles from which the fungus throws out at a favorable moment gelatinous masses of orange-colored spores (Fig. 4 *b*). No fruit of the cedar are apples such as these, fruit rather of the cedar's malignant foe.

Trees are sometimes seen whose crop of "apples" becomes so heavy that disaster almost to extinction marks successive years. Strange to say, the cedar does not bear its affliction alone. The hawthorn has a part in the matter, and on its leaves are borne fringed cups of fungal fruit supplemental to the cedar's parasite, just as the cluster-cups on the barberry-leaves are congeners of the rusts on fields of standing grain.

In fact, with these microscopic forms parasitism is the rule, whether as affecting the vegetable world as we have seen, or in more insidious guise assailing the animal as well, when bacteria and bacilli in phantom myriads appear to baffle surgery and sanitary science. Here, as has been well said, is "the arrow that flieth by day; the pestilence that walketh at noonday." The discussions of a decade have rendered these organisms familiar, at least by name, to every reader. Every wise physician is an experimenter in the field. A new literature has grown up, to which the scientific world makes daily contributions, and bacteriology is hailed the latest phase of biologic science. Nevertheless, the subject is as yet only touched upon. We have simply begun to find out how to study these minutest forms, some of which may yet be hiding beyond our utmost microscopic vision. But the most remarkable group of fungoid organisms remains yet to be considered—remarkable alike because of the innate novelty and beauty of the objects themselves, and because of the difficulty which seems ever likely to attend any effort to fix exactly their place in classification. Among English writers the organisms in question are called slime-molds; in science they have received as a group different appellations.

The slime-molds are sufficiently common in all the wooded regions of the globe, although receiving less attention on account of minuteness and unobtrusiveness.

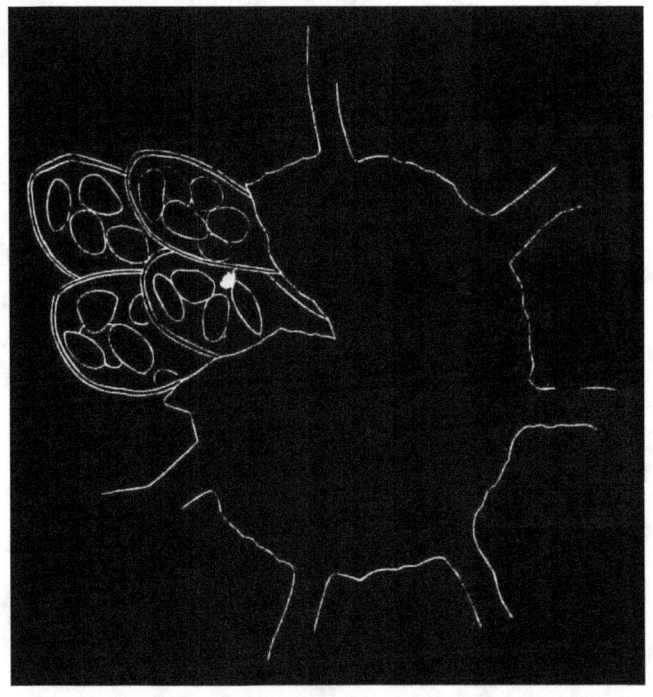

FIG. 1.—FRUIT OF LILAC BLIGHT, X 300.

With most of the species it is a plain case of "*seek* and thou shalt find." Some, however, are quite large, as, for instance, one of the simplest appearing often in summer flowing up between the planks of our familiar board walks, for be it understood at the outset that the slime-molds are, in one stage hi least, soft, protoplasmic bodies possessed of locomotive powers, changing form with protean incertitude, and position with nonchalance far from reassuring.

The species in question appears then, in quantity, a patch of brownish, frothy-looking matter, not attractive. Scrape it away, and probably more will take its place, furnished forth from the moist, dark chambers underneath. Leave it a few hours, and you return to find a mass of purplish dust, overarched, perchance, by a porous crust of yellowish color and fragile structure. This dust is fruit, spores we may say, and we wonder what may be the destiny of spores formed in so strange a fashion.

Place a few of these spores in a moist chamber, and in a short time each germinates and produces—a mycelial thread? Not at all; on the contrary, a protoplasmic particle, not to be distinguished from that other protoplasmic bit men call Amœba. When these Amoebae, produced by the germinating spores, have for a time pursued each his individual way, all under favoring circumstances reassemble, coalesce, actually blending, in most cases, to produce a new slime-mold in all respects comparable to its polymorphic ancestry, a new motile organism ready once more to break up into spores and fruit, and so continue its never-ending cycle of purposeless existence. I say purposeless, for there seems to be no outlet, no outlook toward anything better or higher. Its relations look backward, not forward, and we connect it with the lowest forms of animal life more easily than with anything else. Hence the difficulty of the systematist. Animals they can hardly be, for nowhere else in the kingdom are animals reproduced by spores, to say nothing of the forms of fruiting described later on. We call them for convenience fungi; yet, while some fungi are destitute of mycelium, and some produce swarm spores or motile naked amœboid spores, still in no instance do these behave as in the slime-mold.

FIG. 2.

It is interesting to notice the gingerly manner in which naturalists in their discussions approach these forms. Sachs throws in a chapter, nowhere in particular, a sort of addendum on *Myxomycetes*.

De Bary, the lamented, gives us his masterpiece on fungi, "*including* the *Mycetozoa,*" and in speaking of their relationship says, "For various reasons, which, according to the knowledge at hand, have from time to time been more or less closely worked out, I have, since 1858, placed the *Myxomycetes* (slime-molds) under the name Mycetozoa outside the vegetable kingdom, and this I still consider their proper place." He does not call the organisms *animals,* be it observed.

If a zoölogist chooses to do so, De Bary makes no objection. Meanwhile, Saville

Kent, zoölogist, encouraged probably by De Bary's position, comes forward in his "Manual of Infusoria" and claims the whole series as animals; while Cooke, as representing the English botanists, says, in the introduction to "Myxomycetes of Great Britain," "It is unnecessary to attempt any controversion of the proposition once made, but soon ignored, that these organisms are more intimately related to animals than plants." And Saccardo, in his great work now appearing, "Sylloge Fungorum," enumerates and describes the *Myxomycetes* with the rest.

But while systematists thus differ as to the place the slime-molds should have in classification, we need not hesitate to enjoy their beautiful forms. They are, whether we know what they are or not.

Fig. 3.

54

The sidewalk species is very strange, and the transition from slime to dusty spores would be incredible did we not witness it. Stranger still, however, is the case of a species often brought in midsummer from the woods.

Here, as the object comes from the forest, is a mass of yellowish slime without apparent structure or parts, "without form or comeliness." We lay it upon the laboratory table, shut it up in a box, if you choose, and a few days later examine to find no end of structure. Every particle appears to have passed into the composition of definite and elegant machinery.

A perfect honey-comb now lies upon the bit of rotten wood, the original support, each cell capped with a filmy lid which seems all too fragile, and which, opening here and there, discloses a powdery, fluffy mass within. Brought to the microscope, the contents of each cell spread out in fruit, in spores and banded filaments, "elaters" called, to whose beauty our drawing (Fig. 5) pays but distant tribute.

Golden is the color, sculptured are the spores, and twisted are the filaments with many a delicate spiral wound, the coils running transverse to certain finer striæ, as if the whole structure did but make appeal to some aesthetic eye. Slime-mold it was before, *Trichia chrysosperma* now, and, so far as may be seen, simple evaporation has wrought the change.

Fig. 6 illustrates the fruit of another slime-mold which, during the present year, has been extremely common in this vicinity. Abundant rains during the summer were, perchance, the stimulating cause.

FIG. 4.—"CEDAR-APPLE" AND SPORES—the latter
highly magnified.

On oak-stumps of four or five years' standing there appeared glistening patches of the size of one's hand, by no means attractive to the casual observer; rather the reverse.

Presently the entire mass heaped itself up, becoming, say, four tenths of an inch in depth; a thin film covered all, and desiccation began. Shortly the entire mass had been transformed. Hundreds of slender columnar receptacles, each mounted upon the most delicate little, black, shining pedicle or stalk, and crowded with spores, completely replaced that mass of slime, leaving scarcely a trace.

The upper film breaks away, and a thousand delicate, plume-like structures wave a diminutive forest (Fig. 6). Each tiny stalked receptacle is a spore-case with lacelike walls of richest color, and is at first packed with unicellular sporules of the same deep tint. The entire fruit resembles somewhat a stamen, hence the name, *Stemonitis* (like a stamen). Other fungi, of the same type as left or right floating image with optional over or under description stemonitis, only more delicate still both in form and color, are not infrequent. They are everywhere in the woodland—on leaves and sticks that lie close upon the ground, upon a thousand humblest things. Such forms are the *Comatrichæ, Arcyriæ, Cribrariæ,* etc.

FIG. 5.—SPORES AND ELATERS OF TRICHIA
CHRYSOSPERMA. Highly magnified.

The arcyrias form their spores and the net which contains them all in a delicate spherical or obconical receptacle.

At maturity the upper part breaks away and the elasticity of the contained structures forces them out as a most airy puff, from which the spores may be driven by the wind while the base of the original envelope remains as an empty cup.

Sometimes the entire structure is mounted upon a slender, polished stalk of appreciable length, and the whole colony of sporangia stand as tiny salvers whose shadowy contents rise like incense-wreaths. To find a rosy field of *Arcyria puniceum,* to safely box it and lodge it in one's collection, is enough to give a man joy, even of the aesthetic sort, from Sunday to Sunday.

The tints in all these fruits are just right: they are the grays, the olives, the brick-reds, the browns, and yellows.

Of these that produce their fruit thus in spherical or cup-shaped receptacles, some are giants among the rest. One, very common, imitates the *Lycoperdons,* or puff-balls, and that so closely as to have deceived the botanists themselves. It has been named *Lycoperdon* again and again, and even carried over the whole tribe with which it is related into the order *Gasteromycetes*—the puff-ball order.

The student finds a row of little spheres, ashy or rosy in color, about as large as bullets, resting side by side on some bit of rotten stuff in the woods, and forth-with thinks about *Lycoperdon pusillum,* or possibly some new species, and not until after much investigation and groping, and probably some outside assistance, does he at length reach the "true inwardness" of *Lycogala.*

The more we study these wonderful organisms, the more surprising it seems that two such very different phases should coexist in the same organism and succeed each other so abruptly. We no longer wonder at the perplexity of the systematists, and we can but admire the reckless courage of Saccardo, who discusses the slime-molds in his volume vii, "Sylloge Fungorum" along with other myceliumless forms, and says-never so much as "By your leave."

FIG. 6.—STEMONITIS FUSCA. Central figure x 2;
detail and spores more highly magnified.

Before the vision of the biologist there rises ever more that weird limbo where "*men*" appear "as-*trees* walking." Whether, as in that elder case, experience may bring clearer vision, time alone can tell. Plant and animal have doubtless somewhere a common starting-ground. Toward that common origin the *Myxomycetes* undoubtedly point.

They are not it. They seem rather to represent an independent twig near the base of the great tree of life, a branchlet whose departure was absolute as ancient, developing with no respect to any other organic thing, and soon reaching the limit of that particular possibility. Perfect in themselves, we may look for nothing further in that direction. Nature herself has written, "No thoroughfare."

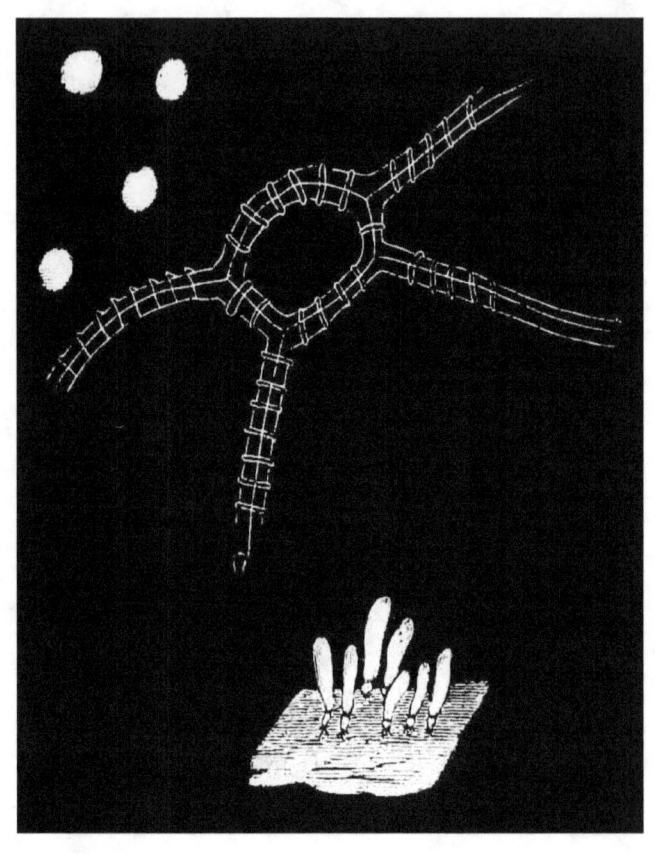

FIG. 7.—ARCYRIA PUNICEA. Detail and spores
highly magnified.

In conclusion, we may notice the question of utility which doubtless rises in some minds. To what end are all these microscopic bits of stuff organic thus hidden from ordinary ken? To such a query no real answer can be given.

Our systems of economics are nowhere sufficiently refined, our tests of value show no balances whose delicacy trembles to a case like this. What know we of Nature's infinite equipoise? Such organisms are their own excuse for being, and, if by any chance they serve at length the aesthetic sense of some creature intellectual, his is the good fortune; their destiny waxes not nor wanes.